The Unbalancing Act
By Kristen Lynn

Plus Bonus Material:
The Vada Diaries, Short Stories and Confessions of a
Crazy Mother

"For my boys and my husband...
Who I love and who drive me crazy."

Contents

The Breaking Point

It was the day from hell. The kind of day where you question whether you should even go to sleep, because you know that you are going to have to get right back up the next morning and start all over again. It was the kind of day where you want to start breaking dishes and cussing out little old ladies. This may sound familiar to you, but for me, this day changed my life.

As a stay-at-home mother of three I followed my normal routine. I got up, fed my kids the most healthful breakfast they would eat, which happened to be frozen waffles and chocolate milk.

By the way, if you are one of those mothers who get up and make spinach and mango smoothies for your children and they suck it right down and then beg you for a broccoli dessert, well, you can pretty much piss off. No offense. I'm happy for you, but maybe a little bitter. I feed my kids what they will eat so they will survive. Don't call the cops on me yet; I do give them a gummy vitamin. Realistically, it is probably way more time and cost efficient and just as healthy as the smoothie bullshit, so don't judge me.

Anyway, I fed my kids, got their teeth brushed, got them dressed, and out the door as we normally do. Only on this particular day, there was no school, some in-service crap or something like that. I have a first grader. I have a kindergartner. I have an eighteen-month-old. Their names are Ben, Max, and Jordan, in that order. All of them are boys. I repeat: all of them are boys. I was so excited we would all get to spend the day together. I had come up with a plan of "Mommy and her little buddies" time. We were going to make memories that would last a lifetime. Well, maybe it wasn't that dramatic, but at least it was something to get us out of the house for a while so they wouldn't destroy it.

It was a Friday. I was cruising down suburbia in a gray mini-van with not just one, but two DVD players, because that's what's up. The boys didn't know where we were going, but they were eager to find out. It was a little chilly outside, chilly enough that our fun was going to have to be an indoor activity. I had discovered this hidden gem of a children's museum and thought the kids would love it. What a good mom I was trying to be. We were going to do something educational and fun on a non-school day. That's me though, I always strive for perfection and most often come up short. However, I always try the shit out of it.

We live in a suburb of Kansas City, on the Kansas side. A town of mini-vans, SUV's (which are necessary for the flat lands of Kansas' bumpy terrain, yeah right) and show cars. You know, the ones that have the same engines under the hoods as all the rest, but you pay twenty thousand more for the luxury name. You know what I'm talking about. I'm not judging. I'm just speaking the truth. As far as motherhood goes, it's the best thing that has ever happened to me. I am, however, on antidepressants, and I am a total fucked up mess. My internal dialogue and what actually comes out of my mouth are two totally different things. It's almost like leading a double life. But we'll get into that later. Let me get back to this particular day.

We pulled into the museum parking lot. "Here we are!" I turned and told the kids.

Ben immediately started bawling. Max growled, "Aww...great. This place?"

"You don't even know where we are! Why are you complaining?" I asked.

"Because we didn't want to go to a stupid school! There is no school today, Mom! You are the meanest Mom I ever had!" cried Ben.

They had a point. This museum was in a brick building with small windows and it looked just like a school. I did my best to explain to them that it was a fun place. It's not like a "school" it's more like place to explore things and do activities, no homework. They would have been fine if I'd have taken them to a Pantera concert. My kids are so crazy. They literally love 80's hair bands and metal, especially power ballads. They have big futures waiting for them in the music industry. I just hope they remember to thank their mommy in all of their award speeches.

After convincing them to at least come in and try it or we can all just "go home and go straight to bed for the rest of the night" at ten o'clock in the morning, I used my automatic hatch opener to get my stroller out of the back. Let me tell you, at that moment I almost ran out in front of a car. I wanted to. Not to die, just to have an ambulance put me on a stretcher and take me away. I had forgotten the motherfucking stroller. This left me with some options, I could either go twenty minutes back home and get it, or take an eighteen-month-old maniac into a children's museum with two other children on foot. I was not going back home. I could do this, right? I wasn't going to let three little kids intimidate me. No way in hell. Looking back, I probably should have gone with my first instinct and got hit by a car.

We walked in holding hands, and stopped at the front desk to pay. For me and my three angels, the admission fee was forty-eight dollars. I almost told the museum staff to take their "educational exploration" and stick it up their asses, but seeing as we had made it that far, I paid it. I really did at least expect a voucher for a free fingering from a hot firefighter while a background-checked nanny guided my children through the facility. Forty-eight dollars my ass! Anyways, moving on...

I was holding Jordan. Max and Ben were holding hands and we went to the first exhibit. It was a room full of blocks. They stayed entertained and I was able to let Jordan down to play, so I figured this was a good room for us to be in. They built towers and castles and they cried every time Jordan knocked their buildings down. I finally got sick of holding back my little demolition man, and we decided to move on to the next room. We visited the dinosaur bones exhibit, and then explored the arts and crafts room where I was helping baby Jordan to color on construction paper. I looked over at the easel Max was working on, and he had beautifully painted a giant cock and balls with green paint. In fact, it was a pretty accurate painting. Even one ball was droopier than the other. The other mothers in the room looked at me in disgust and I told them to fuck off. Not really, but I wanted to. I simply said, "Oh my! Max, your mommy is not going to like you drawing things like that! What am I going to tell her when she picks you up today?" Max looked at me like I was crazy, but just moved on to his next project. He was catching on that I sometimes play it off like I am just the babysitter when they embarrass me in public.

Moving down the hall of the museum from room to room, Jordan was getting squirmy and would no longer let me hold him. After feeling like I had wrestled an alligator and lost the match, I decided to let him walk. Big mistake! No, huge mistake! He took off running through the crowded hall as a toddler normally would; only it was like he had nitrous oxide boosters on his teeny tiny shoes. Of course I ran after him yelling his name, but he just kept going. I would have caught up quicker if everyone had just gotten the hell out of my way. I finally caught him.

"No! No! Jordan!" I said. "You do not run away from mommy!"

It was then, that he smacked me in the face and yelled "No! No!" In other words, he simply told me "shut up bitch." I picked him up and turned around to tell the other boys it was time to go and that I'd had enough. There was a big problem. They were nowhere in sight. I immediately panicked. My heart was racing and all I could do was run, searching and yelling, "I lost my boys! I lost my boys!" I must have looked in every room. A group of sympathetic mothers had joined my search team. We were all calling out their names and suddenly a light bulb went off— the bathroom! I ran as fast as I could into the bathroom and my panic turned into sobbing tears as I saw four little feet in the handicapped stall. They were giggling. I set Jordan down and went to hug them even though I was so angry. I was scared shitless and yet just elated they were safe.

"Don't you ever leave on your own like that again, do you hear me?" I said, still crying.

The boys were completely unaware until they saw my tears that anything was even wrong. Their innocent faces looked at me with sincere remorse.

"I'm sorry, Mommy," said Ben, "Max had to poop."

Max apologized as well, and I felt so lucky that they were safe, at that point none of it really mattered. I stuck my head out the door and yelled down the hall that they had been found so that the search team could call off their efforts. I heard giggles behind me and a "Holy crap" from Ben's mouth. I turned around to see what may have been the only thing worse than losing the boys that day. My baby Jordan was splashing around in the toilet in another stall...and it hadn't been flushed.

Let's just say this was a breaking point for me. The thought of (I can't even say the word) "fecal" eww...matter and urine on my child's hands sent me into a personal hell that you cannot imagine. Having three boys, I'm used to gross things. However, I don't do odors. I don't do little hairs. I most certainly do not do bodily fluids. Of course, my own children's poopy diapers and things like that don't bother me, but someone else's sure fucking does.

After this horrific incident, I stripped Jordan naked and washed his whole body with soap in the bathroom sink. I made my big boys scrub their hands until the soap ran out and then we went straight home and everyone got a bath. I needed to regroup. I was so stressed out that every single muscle in my body hurt from being so tense. I called my husband Eric and told him what had happened. He responded like it was no big deal and that the kids were going to be fine. He told me that I needed to calm down. You know what I thought? That motherfucker wasn't even there, so how can he tell me to calm down? I gently placed him on my shit list and put Jordan down for a nap. He'd been scrubbed so clean that his skin literally squeaked. I put on a movie for Max and Ben and went to get the mail.

After jiggling the mail key, which is finicky like everything else in my life, and opening up the silver box, I grabbed the mail stack with two hands. There it was, on top of the pile of bills and junk mail, a brochure for the New Outlook Center for Mental and Behavioral Health that Eric had requested online. After a series of events that had happened over the last several months, he thought I should seek some counseling to deal with some stress and anxiety issues. I always brushed him off. I was already on antidepressants for heaven's sake. The facility was only about thirty minutes south of our suburban paradise in a small town called Rivergate. I had to laugh because I really felt like I was going nuts and here was this brochure. Maybe it was a sign. As I looked through the pages, I saw happy-looking crazy women. They looked like ordinary soccer moms. Looking back now, I'm sure they used models for the photographs in the brochure. The place seemed quite lovely, like a retreat. There was a spa, recreational activities, walking trails, and medication. Oh my! If only I would have known...

Jordan's nap was short and the boys grew bored of movie time fairly quickly. It was barely enough time for me to get my floors mopped and the dishwasher unloaded. By three o'clock in the afternoon, I was already ready for bed. Eric called to say he'd be working late. Hooray for me! I took the three boys down to the playroom and told them to play a board game, Candyland. Who doesn't like Candyland, right? The game began and I had to hold Jordan back because he had no interest in doing anything other than destroying their game board. It was almost like watching a freak show. Ben and Max kept blaming each other for cheating, when in reality, they were both cheating.

"Play fair you guys, or we are not playing anything at all!" I warned in my scary mom voice.

Once Max pulled the ice cream card out from under his leg (where he was hiding it) and got to move his green game piece all the way to the top of the board, Ben lost it and sucker punched him right in the lip. It bled. It bled like crazy. Everyone was crying, even Jordan. I put them all in the van, each one bawling their eyes out. My knuckles were white as I gripped the steering wheel. I was so tense that I probably looked like a giant praying mantis driving my mini-van down the street. I drove to the first place I could think of, our city's juvenile detention center. I parked and turned off the engine. Things grew quieter, but I could still hear a few sniffles.

"Where are we, Mommy?" asked Max.

"Mommy, what are we doing?" cried Ben.

I looked in the back seat and saw my three boys staring at me in horror. Actually, Jordan was chewing on his toes and couldn't have cared less where we were, but my big boys were terrified.

"Do you see this building right here?" I asked.

They nodded.

"This is called juvie, short for juvenile detention." I said, "This is jail...for kids. This is where kids have to go when they break the law. When they punch people, or cheat, or steal, the police take them here!" I looked at Ben, "You gave your brother a bloody lip today, Ben. Do you think that's okay?"

"Noooooo!" he wailed.

"Cheating is like stealing Max, do you think that's okay?"

"Stop it, Mommy....noooo....I'm sorry, Mommy, I'm sorry!" Max cried.

I was starting to feel bad, but after the day I had, I wasn't backing down yet. "Do you boys understand that if you don't stop acting this way and hitting each other and fighting that you could have to be in here one day? In handcuffs? The only food they have in there is vegetables and meat and they make you drink tomato juice." Threatening them with healthy food...I add that to my list of reasons I should be nominated for Mother of the Year.

"Mommy!!! Pleeease take us home! We will never fight again. We will do whatever you say. Please don't take us to jail. Jordan's just a baby! How can you do this to a little baby?" cried Ben.

"Well, get a good look boys because I never, *ever* want to have to drive into this parking lot again. Do you understand me?"

"Yes, Mommy!" they both replied. They looked so relieved.

I turned the car back on and headed for home, which was, unfortunately, the last place I wanted to go. It felt like we'd been cooped up for so long. Kansas weather is so up and down. In the beginning of spring, one day it's hot and sticky, the next day it's cold and cloudy. The nice days were coming soon; they were still playing peek-a-boo at that point. The boys stopped crying as we pulled into the driveway. Max undid his seatbelt and came up and hugged me.

"We forgive you, Mommy," he said.

I hoped that he was just confusing his words, but probably not. I think he thought I should really be sorry.

My cell rang. It was my mother. After explaining my day, she offered to have them stay at her house for the night. I immediately and thankfully agreed. I love them so much, but I was so stressed out that I needed some quiet time and I know they loved staying with her. It was a win-win. She told me to bring them over whenever they were ready. I quickly packed their bags.

Before we left, I kissed each of them and told them how sorry I was that we had a rough day. I explained to them that I wanted them to be good listeners so that they would have a better day tomorrow and the next day and each day after that. They must have "forgiven" me, because I got lots of hugs and cuddles. I threw their bags and overnight things in the back hatch of my mini-van, buckled Jordan into his car seat, climbed into the driver's seat, and put the car in reverse.

"Hey little buddies, are you guys excited about going to Grandma's house?" I asked. "Make sure you..."

SCREEEEEECHHHH!

I heard this awful noise because I fucking hit the top of the garage door. I forgot to close the back hatch. I tried to pull forward and again heard the sound of grinding metal. I remember thinking to myself that this day was going to be the end of me. I think every single cuss word in every language in the world went through my mind at the same time. I stepped out to assess the damage.

It didn't look as bad as it had sounded and I managed to get the hatch to shut, but the garage door wouldn't close. There were scratches all over the back of my mini-van, but I didn't really care because it's a mini-van. Enough said. I called my mother in tears and told her the situation.

"I'll be right there to get them!" she said.

She was there within fifteen minutes. We loaded them up in her car and holding back more tears, I told them all I would pick them up in the morning and bring them a surprise. I was trying to compensate for blowing our whole day by being a total freak. They waved good-bye and I remember standing there in my hooded sweatshirt trying to figure out how I was going to tell Eric that I had broken the damn garage door.

He is a great guy, usually pretty laid-back, not the kind of guy to flip out over something like that. It's just that I felt like such a nipple for doing it. What was I going to say when he got home from work? "Oh, hey honey, today after I lost our kids and exposed the baby to hepatitis, I took the kids to juvie and then crashed the van into our garage door. How was your day darling?" I decided even though I was freezing my balls off, I was going to get the garage door to shut. The opener was not working, so I pulled the little red string that unhooks the automatic and tried to pull it down with my muscles. I had to get a chair so I could reach, and after lots and lots of maneuvering and cussing, I got it to go down. I swear if my neighbors would have heard the words that were coming out of my mouth, they'd have called the cops. At one point, and I'm ashamed to admit this, I told the garage door to go and fuck it's mother's ass. Who the hell says that? At least it finally went down. Even though I knew I was going to eventually have to tell Eric, I could at least maybe stall the conversation until tomorrow. Fortunately, he parks in the driveway anyway.

I walked back into the house and collapsed on the couch. All was quiet. My house is so much different when it's quiet, like a store that's closed. I never know what to do when I am alone. I usually clean, but I forced myself to sit still and give myself a minute. I had left the brochure for the New Outlook Center on the coffee table. The extremely jovial and yet supposedly mentally ill woman on the cover was staring at me, smiling. I covered it up with a magazine and laid down for a grand total of five minutes before Eric's key turned in the front door. He hugged me hello and asked where the kids were. When I told him they were at my mom's for the night, he gave me that look. The look that basically means, "There is no excuse for not having sex." Oh bloody hell.

Eric and I have had a happy marriage. We've been faithful and good to each other for thirteen years, married for seven. He can piss me off quicker than anyone I've ever met, though. He usually does it on purpose. He's clumsy and sweet and means well. He spills everything. Literally every beverage the man has ever carried has been spilled in one way or another. Coffee, soda, you name it. I can usually find him anywhere in the house by following his drips from one room to another, because he is always spilling as he walks. He is one thirsty sonofabitch too, because he always has a drink in his hand. He doesn't drink alcohol much, though, which is probably one of the reasons we mesh so well. I always have a designated driver. I even blame his spillage on my last pregnancy. It wasn't planned, but Eric spilled a little on the way out. I knew immediately and said, "Oh great! I felt that, you idiot, now I'm pregnant. Way to go genius." Bam...two weeks later I was "late," bought a drug store brand pregnancy test, and saw a plus sign. It's the one spill I'm glad he made, because I don't know what I'd do without my baby Jordan. He was meant to be. So I have learned to accept his spills and keep my mop handy at all times. I also made him get a vasectomy...immediately.

He threw his backpack down on the floor, which always bothers me for two reasons. First of all, it should be put in the closet. And secondly, it has his computer in it and I'm always afraid he's going to break it. He immediately walked over and put his arms around me. Not so much in a "honey I'm home" way, but more of an "I'm as hard as a rock" way. He took my hand and led me upstairs. I followed along like a child being dragged to time-out. I couldn't even imagine doing sex things at that point. I just wanted to be left alone. I had to go along, because it wasn't his fault my day had been so shitty, but I still didn't want to do it. He unzipped my hoodie, which for me, at home, is like lingerie. As per usual, one hand went to a boob, the other hand went to the kitty cat.

"Eric, I don't know if I can do this right now. My allergies are killing me!" I said very apologetically.

He looked at me with that little disappointed look he gets. "Well, I'm not going to stick it in your nose Vada," he said, "unless you just want me to."

I had to laugh. "Well, I have a headache and I'm not sure I'll be very good at it. I'll probably be better at it tomorrow. I'm probably going to just lay there like a dead person. Wouldn't you rather wait until tomorrow? Or perhaps I could call you a prostitute? Would you like that? I'll pick you out a real nice one with big boobs and daddy issues?"

"Vada, you're the only hooker I want to have sex with so take some allergy medicine and quit bitching."

"Oh fucking fine!" I snapped. "But at least let me take a shower first and brush my teeth. Don't say I didn't warn you that I'm going to be a dead lay! And remember this is against my will!"

"I'll risk it, now hurry up."

14

I showered, brushed my teeth, and put on a bra, underwear, and a t-shirt.

"Why do you always do that?" he asked. "You know I'm just going to take it off you anyways."

"Why don't you worry about what you are doing and quit worrying about what I'm doing? Mind your own business."

I crawled into bed and did the best I could, considering the circumstances. Fortunately, he had to make it quick because he had a work call to get on, so it was short and sweet and to the point. It's what I like to call a "quick hit." That's my favorite kind. It's kind of like walking into a casino and hitting a jackpot with your first twenty bucks. It was just in this case I was the machine and he was the money. Ding ding ding, now cash out. You got what you came for, time to move along.

We laid there for a minute afterwards. I remember Eric asking me about my day and if it had gotten any better since our phone conversation. All I could say was, "Nothing really exciting happened." I simply did not want to get into it. What I did want was a glass of wine. I had some hidden in the laundry room. Weird, huh? I know, but like I said before, don't judge me. I poured a glass. He said he had to jump on his call, so I took advantage and sat in peace and drank wine. It was a nice relaxing moment.

I'm a drink-smoker. That means I only smoke when I drink. Two sips or two hundred sips, I immediately want to smoke the minute alcohol touches my lips. This is something Eric does not approve of. He hates the smell and just doesn't get it. Well...he can suck it, because that is just the way I am and there is nothing I can do to change it. After the day I had, I thought I deserved a nice relaxing smoke with my nice relaxing wine.

I remembered that I had a pack of cigs hidden in an old purse in my bedroom closet. I went and fetched them. It was too cold to go outside and so I thought I'd sneak into the garage. I tried to manually lift the garage door, the same door that I had earlier suggested incestuous sodomy to, but it would only budge a crack. I thought a crack was good enough, and I was freezing. I decided I would sit in my van and blow the smoke out the window. I climbed in the van and turned it on to roll the window down. I lit my stogie and turned on my heated seats, carefully blowing the vapors out of the window as not to taint the car with the smell. I was enjoying my nicotine and spirits, which were finally beginning to lift my spirits, when I heard a beeping noise. Eric came running out yelling my name.

"Vada! Oh my God! The carbon monoxide detector is going off. What the hell are you doing? Turn the car off! You're going to kill yourself!"

I seriously didn't realize I had turned the engine on. I only meant to turn it enough to power the automatic windows and warm my butt up. I knew at that moment I was screwed, quite literally in the hot seat. Eric forced the garage door up enough and cleared the air out. He made me leave the house with him and had the firemen come make sure it was safe. Once they said it was, we went back into the house and he was acting funny. I can't really explain it, but it was like he was worried and wanted to talk to me about something but he couldn't. When we laid down for bed he started to rub my back. I thought that meant I was going to have to give it up again. Normally, his hands usually find their way around to the front, only this time they didn't.

"Vadie," he said, "we need to talk."

Doing the Mom Thing

If you are reading this, there is probably a chance that you just got your kids down to sleep and you have a small window of time before someone needs to pee, or has a bad dream, or a baby starts to cry. Congratulations! You have accomplished an amazing thing. You have managed to satisfy a basic human need that often goes unmet once you have reproduced. Also, if you are reading this, there is probably a chance that you are using your "me time," which has become almost non-existent since you have procreated.

Many of your basic human needs have most likely been forgotten since the moment your precious darling or darlings entered this world. Among these is the need to eat, sleep, and take a piss or shit in private, which is now considered a luxury experience. Since becoming a parent, you have given up the rights to your body and appearance. Your boobies may have had the life sucked right out of them. Your once tight ass is wider and more unfortunate than ever before. Your hair may go up wet and then frizz by noon, giving you a battered wife look. On the other hand, it may just have to be covered by a ball cap that itches like hell and will smell like dead mouse when you take it off.

Let's address sexy time. I'm sure that's important to you in one way or another. That's a completely normal human activity, right? What used to be lights-on naughty-nighty on the kitchen counter humping, has now turned into the mission for missionary covered from head to toe with a comforter and one eye on the door with an overwhelming fear that your child will walk in and be scarred for life. Worse than that is the fear of actually getting into it enough that you start feeling something down there only to be cut off by a wail on the baby monitor leaving you with a case of female blueballs. Your man is gonna take care of his own business while you go down and get the baby back to sleep. Blah. You may want to just forget about it in the first place.

Let me add that while you have lost all of these things, these rights, these needs, you *have* gained the world. The fact that you have signed over your life doesn't mean it's all for nothing. As parents, we know that it is all worth it. Our babies, our families are worth every bit of sacrifice. We are martyrs. We are warriors. We are mothers. And although we may look like we have nothing left in us by the end of the day, there is still enough left in us to fight for our "me time." So when you win this battle and you have this precious little ounce of time, try not to waste it. Read a book, watch those Kardashians, or just go eat your kids' Halloween candy and say fuck a lot. It's your time, so make it count.

Thanks as always for reading!
~V-Bow

March 2nd

    That's my blog, by the way. I have a blog. I use "V-Bow" as my name because I try and remain somewhat anonymous. My blogs aren't exactly PG, and I don't need judgment. I can't handle it. This post is kind of special to me for some reason. It's actually the last post I wrote before I got to this place. I kept having these little ideas, stories, and thoughts and I would randomly jot them down and email them to my friends and family. After a hundred times of hearing, "You should start a blog" I just did it. Being a stay-at-home mom, I found some time at least once or twice a week to share my funny stories or my ideas and at least let the world out there know I was alive. It's been going okay and I guess I feel better having a blog, than being blog-less, if that makes any sense at all. It's like, okay, today I am going to do something with myself, besides housework, and carpool, and trying to be the best mommy in the whole wide world. I don't have a huge following, but enough to keep writing. So, that's why I blog.

    I am thirty-one. I'm okay with the thirty, but the one part throws me off for some reason. I can't figure out why. Maybe I don't like odd numbers or maybe it's just that I'm older than thirty. I really am a nice girl, I swear. I participate in every school function, I never miss a well-visit at the pediatrician, and I literally mop my floors three times each day. Clean floors make me feel in control. They make me feel like I am doing a good job, even if the kids are screaming and we are running late, and I have fly-aways hanging out from my pony tail, like Shelly Duvall in *The Shining*. I mean what if the president stopped by? Wouldn't you want to have clean floors? Well, I would, whether it was George W. Bush, Barack Obama, or George Washington, I'd like to have clean floors for the president.

    I wanted kids all my life. I was just sure of it. I had the baby fever so bad that I would dream about babies every night. I would even rock a stuffed teddy bear with a diaper on it sometimes. I guess that is a little nutty, but I'm not in here for nothing. Oh, where am I you ask? I'm in the Nuthouse, The Looney Bin. Yep, that night after the carbon monoxide incident, Eric talked me into it. So here I am at The New Outlook Center for Mental and Behavioral Health, Women's Division. Mrs. Vada Bower.

Complete with an I.D. number and pills that come in little white cups, just like in the movies. My food comes on a little tray. They wake me at seven for breakfast and lights out is at ten. It's slow-paced and quiet, for the most part. I get to take walks and read and watch the other nuts crack several times a day. Mary, my roommate, is crazy...like bath salts crazy. I'm actually afraid she's going to eat my face, so I'm trying to get moved to a private room. It shouldn't be hard because the staff here all know I'm not like these people. I'm afraid if I stay with her for too long, I'll become a crazy-eyed bag of shit too. What if it's contagious? Her way-too-short bangs stick to her forehead and are always damp. Maybe it's because she's sweaty, or maybe she's just greasy. The first two inches of her mangy-looking hair are dishwater blonde and the bottom is dyed jet black. Not an intentional ombre style if you know what I mean. The poor thing's face is so terribly broken out for an adult. I would really like to share some skincare product tips with her, but I'm not sure she would be too open to my help. She doesn't say much, but she doesn't have to. Her eyes are huge and bloodshot and she always looks like she's bearing down—for a crap, or labor, or something. She's not pregnant, but I'm ready for a gremlin baby to pop out of her at any moment. The idea of her looking at me with those eyes and crapping all over our room would probably freak me out more than delivering her baby. I could totally see the little thing coming out and looking up at me with those same eyes. Then, it would probably crap all over me as I tried to cut the cord. It would be my luck to get the best of both worlds. Anyway, I should be getting away from her soon. I may be off my rocker a little, but I'm not crazy.

We are having grilled chicken salad, bread sticks, and a pudding cup for dinner tonight. The pudding cup makes me miss my boys. They love those things and I get to lick the lid. They are always so quick to offer it and always so proud of their own generosity. Mary needs to keep her big bulging eyes on her own damn pudding cup. The way she keeps eye-fucking my dessert makes me not want it and it is really screwing up my nostalgic moment. What a nut bag. I want to dump it in the trash. But it's chocolate. I can't do it. I glare at her to see if she'll blink but she doesn't. My thoughts are racing and I'm getting a little frightened. Alright little Miss Mary Quite Contrary, you wanna go? I'm game. I'll knock the crazy right out of your stupid face. I may be five foot tall and as big as your right thigh, but I know how to fight, because my boys taught me. And I don't fight fair. I'll smack your acne ridden face so hard that all those boils will pop at the same time, so you'd better fetch a rag to catch the drippings. I don't want that shit on the floor. I like clean floors. And by the way, I know you are in here for bipolar disorder, so I really hope it's happy time. That way you can feel all euphoric while I kick the ever-loving piss out of you and then sit on your passed-out body while I eat my dessert. What a psycho. But in real life, I don't say or do any of these things. In fact, I offer her my pudding cup. She takes it without saying a word. So I lie in bed and stew about why I'm so pathetic for the rest of the night. I finally rationalize what I've done by deciding that I'd rather her eat my pudding cup than eat my face.

March 3rd

"You ready for your visitors?" I hear. It's Katelyn, the sweet little nurse who pretends to love her job. I wonder why she doesn't just check herself in with the rest of us. Anyone who is this immaculate in their appearance has got to be covering up some kind of crazy. She is absolutely gorgeous. Her skin is a beautiful, dark brown and her black hair is pulled back in a funky knot with braids crossing in and out of wavy strands. Very boho-perfect. Her make-up is flawless and her complexion makes me feel like I should really start using toner. Her eye make-up I swear has to be tattooed on because it never smudges or fades and you can literally count her thick and separated lashes. She has striking brown eyes and a little heart-shaped smile. She literally looks like she's been photo shopped. I haven't asked but I would guess her to be around thirty or so, my age. I know she can't be as perfect as she looks and she is always sniffling. I can't figure out if she's got seasonal allergies or if she is maybe snorting a little something-something out of those little white cups, if you know what I mean. Something's keeping this chick one hundred pounds and working so fast. If I had to bet on it, I'd bet her allergies are just fine. I like Katelyn.

I head for the visiting room with the big double doors. Today I have my hair up in a high ponytail and I put on a pair of sweats and a pink hoodie. Damn it. If I'm going to be in the insane asylum, I'm going to be comfortable! I can't wait to see my babies! I've only been in here for a few days and I miss them like crazy. The three boys are each holding a flower and they all look happy to see me.

"Hello, my precious angels!" I say and I wrap my arms around all three at the same time. I get lots of hugs and kisses and a sharp pang of guilt tight in my gut and another one of sadness that I have missed out on almost two days of their lives.

I look them up and down and make sure there are no scratches or bruises since I've been away. Since it is still a bit chilly out, they have probably been mostly inside and therefore not getting hurt. They look good and healthy. I finally bring myself to look at my husband.

"Hey you, kid, how are things on the outside?" I ask. I elbow him playfully because I'm not sure how to greet the man I married, who has so strongly expressed his belief that I need professional help.

"Oh Vadie, I am so sorry!" he says. I think a tear comes to his eye and he fights it back for a second. "Are you holding up okay? Are you eating well?"

The questions continue and I answer each of them with as much honesty as I can manage. I quickly turn the subject back to the boys. Looking over at Ben, Max, and Jordan, I can't believe how beautiful they are. Ben has Max in a headlock and Jordan is trying to draw on the wall with the slobber from his binky. Ben has a pretty good grip, and Max can hardly move until he manages to throw an elbow right into the chest of his older brother.

"Ohhhhhhh....you stupid wiener factory!" yells Ben. His big brown eyes immediately look my way and he knows he's said a bad word.

"Mom, tell him he's the wiener factory!" Max sobs and runs over to me. His blue-green eyes are now red with tears, and his face is radiating hot pink heat from a bitch slap that I believe may have occurred before the headlock.

I'd like to tell them that I am actually the wiener factory, since all I can seem to produce are boys. I hug him even though I know they should both be in trouble and I look at my little toddling Jordan baby. He has these great big brown eyes and sweet little brown curls in the back of his hair that I just can't bear to cut off. I always thought that curls looked dumb on boys until it was my kid. It's kind of like ugly newborn babies. They are all kind of like swamp creatures until it's your own and then it's suddenly the most beautiful thing you have ever seen. His curls will stay. Just so we are clear...mine were beautiful newborn babies. Just sayin'.

"Why are you fighting?" I ask. "Now stop that at least while you are here. For goodness sake you should be loving on me with your sweet faces instead of fighting. So knock it off."

This is part of my problem. Eric and I cannot talk. We cannot talk because when we try, our kids will start fighting, or crying, or asking for a drink of water. They will do just about anything to keep our attention on them at all times, and it works. Some mother I am. I've taught my kids letters, numbers, how to ride a bike, how to (poorly) make their beds, you name it. The one thing I have forgotten to teach them is how to shut the hell up. Seriously. That might sound mean, but they can't shut up for one minute. Times that by three. Now, see if that doesn't make you want to fling your shit like a chimp at the zoo. Yikes!

"Boys, would you do me the best and biggest favor and draw me some pictures?" I ask.

This is one of my glorious tactics to get them to stop fighting and calm down. It works. We all sit at the big rectangle table and draw. Eric tells me that nothing has been going on and that things are pretty dull around the house. My mother and his mother have been helping him with the kids. He tells me that he doesn't want me to worry about a thing. I just need to concentrate on taking the time to get better so I can come home strong and healthy and focused. I just smile and change the subject to things like his job and some projects we'll want to start when I get home. At this point the boys are doing fine. Ben has drawn what looks to be a ninja of some kind. Max has a piece of paper with six oval shapes and a vertical line down the middle of each one. I don't have a clue what these are but I don't want to hurt his feelings, so I just smile.

"Your pictures are awesome boys. You guys are the best artists I've ever met and I love everything you make!" I say. They look at me with proud eyes.

"Mommy, what's that smell?" asks Max.

"I don't know baby, maybe Jordan needs a diaper." I check and he's clean. I really don't smell anything, but start to wonder if I am just used to the smell of this place. It's not necessarily bad, kind of smells like a new bandage when you take off the wrapper.

"Can I keep these pictures to hang by my bed so I can look at them when I miss you guys?" They nod. "And Jordan, can I just keep you here with me to use as my pillow?"

The boys all laugh as I take my darling baby and pretend to be asleep and snoring on his tummy. Jordan laughs and I kiss his belly and then his sweet cheeks that smell like baby soap and vanilla wafers. I love that smell.

"But Mommy, don't you smell that?" Max is insisting.

I tell him again that I don't smell anything and after much hugging and kissing and "I love you's," Nurse Katelyn comes in and says I have to go to my group session in five minutes. As I am watching the loves of my life walking towards the door, I blow kisses and tell them I will call them and that I'll be home soon. Max stops and looks up at me. I'm feeling so much guilt and I think he is going to cry for me to go home with them. Oh no! This cannot be happening, because if he has a breakdown, it will kill me and I will have to give this place up and go straight home.

"Mommy…I know what that smell is," he yells with a smile "it's all those butt cracks I drew on your picture."

Nice.

My First Group

It's time to start some "real" therapy. The time I've spent here so have far has been mostly answering questions and filling out forms. Things are about to get a little more complicated now. I head down to the Solarium, which is actually a very beautiful room. They hid it on the back side of the nuthouse so that we can see out, but the curious people who want to get a look at the crazies can't see in. The hospital owns a lot of land behind here, and you can't see anything but nature from inside these walls. The room looks out over a sparkling pond with small, manmade waterfalls on each side. Flowerbeds and birdbaths and cheerful things decorate the courtyard outside. However, I do find it odd that there is a giant weeping willow that almost seems the centerpiece of the landscaping. I mean really? Really…or not? Did it not dawn on any of these people that a weeping willow is a really bad fucking choice? I don't know why this strikes me as such a fail, but you take a bunch of wackos who are depressed, anxious, suffering from post-traumatic stress, and God only knows what else and then put a big weeping willow in the middle of their happy place! You might as well sit us all down to watch a funny movie and put in *Beaches*. Why not just show us all a sweet baby bunny and then feed it to a dog? Geez…but anyway, the room inside is light and airy. Beiges and creams with fresh pink roses and lilies on the tables. The couches are soft and there are even little treats set out, cookies and tea. I get it…but watch out for us bulimic gals. We'll just throw it up anyways, right? That's what this group is. It is the eating disorder one. I'm so excited about it that I could just puke.

The ladies slowly make their way in and we all sit. You can see the ones who are sizing each other up. I could care less about their sizes; I'm just excited about the cookies. There are iced sugar and chocolate chip oatmeal. I'm in heaven. I can't imagine what kind of therapy this will be. Maybe we'll play a team building game and we can toss our cookies! I immediately grab a napkin and start munching. It's not a bit awkward until I hear my name being called and I am still chewing.

"Vada Bower?"

"That's me," I say, trying to swallow fast.

"Would you care to introduce yourself and give us a little background?" says a rather concerned-looking counselor who I have not seen before. She has red-rimmed glasses and a blunt hair cut that sits right at chin level. This lady is small but looks like she means business. She looks at me like I'm going to dart to the ladies room as fast as possible and purge. She's in a stance like she's ready to catch me if I go flying. I wish she would calm the hell down. Her name tag says Rita, and all I can think of is a marga-Rita...on the rocks with salt. I try to focus.

"My name is Vada, but some people call me Vadie. I have three little boys. I just got here two days ago and everyone's been so nice. I'm not sure what to say, but I guess I'm just impressed by the whole place. I really like how clean everything is and it's great to have such beautiful trails and huge trees..."

"Mrs. Bower, I'm glad you are finding your stay here enjoyable, however in this group we are open to hearing more of your personal matters. If you are not ready to share then we will give you a free pass since this is your first session. We find healing to be a group experience. We don't judge, we only listen and learn from one another. I myself am a recovering anorexic and bulimic, and I still struggle with staying healthy every day. However, it's a fight I've been winning for six years now. Are you ready? Would you like to share with us your issues?" asks Rita.

All I keep thinking is,
RitaRitaBoBitaBananaFanaFoFitaMeMyMoMitaRita.

"Mrs. Bower?"

"Umm...yes. I have issues. I definitely have issues," I say.

I decide to take my free pass and they are onto the next girl. She's a tall, stick-thin, and pretty little thing named Jessalyn who's got to be about twenty-five or so. She begins to tell her story about how she's been anorexic since she was thirteen. She started having problems with food after being molested by a sick, disgusting, pervert of a grandfather. She says that keeping that secret has caused her to be obsessed with being in control of her body. As I listen to this poor girl go into detail about her daily routine of avoiding anything to do with food, it makes me sad. She goes on about becoming socially withdrawn and has isolated herself from friends and family. I mean this poor girl. What an awful way to live.

I cannot relate to what Jessalyn has been through, but I think I understand her. The group continues and I hear other numerous stories from these ladies who all have reasons for hacking twenty times a day, or not eating at all, and some of them even both. Each one of them is an eye opener for me. The truth to my story is not as dramatic. The truth to my story is this:

One day this winter, I got into all the kids leftover Christmas candy. I ate a solid chocolate Santa, four of those delicious little peanut butter and chocolate Christmas trees, a piece of cherry pie, about a half a pound of cinnamon bears, and then I needed something salty so I made popcorn. I ate it. I had never in my life eaten so much and I felt like I was ready to blow. I thought about it for a second, and had what I felt was an epiphany. Why don't I go puke this shit up and pretend like it never happened? That's right. I'll just start puking after I eat and then I don't have to worry about the rest of this baby weight, it will fall right off! Brilliant! Why hadn't I thought of this before?

Now look, I am not body obsessed, but I am body conscious and I gained sixty pounds with my third pregnancy. I ate everything I could get my mouth around. I am normally about one hundred and ten pounds so you can bet I looked like I was a reflection in a funhouse mirror when I was nine months along. Even my eyelids were fat. My nose spread so far that the skin on it looked like an orange peel from my pores being stretched so far. I still have a few pounds to lose to fit into my "goal jeans" but for crying out loud, I've come a long way. Besides, I learned after my first baby, even if the weight comes off, the body parts don't always shift back to the same place.

Anyway, my two big boys were at school and the baby was napping. I went in to the toilet and of course wiped all the boys piss off with spray and paper towels to prepare for my glorious purging event. I stuck my finger down my throat and nothing happened. I did it again, further this time. What the hell! Why wasn't this working? I thought it was my stance so I put one leg up on the toilet and gave a big poke down the back of my throat. Up came a gigantic gag…just a loud gag…but still no treats. I tried again, just a dry heave, and again the same thing. I shot a glance at myself in the mirror. My eyes were red and teary from the gagging and my face burned. I learned that I was the loudest non-puking-puker ever to walk the earth. I also decided, fuck this shit, the baby is going to wake up any minute and I haven't accomplished a thing except now I feel shitty. Right then and there I had decided this bulimia thing was not for me. First of all, I suck at it, and second of all, I just plain don't have the time for it. I wiped my eyes, and then I saw a figure move in the hallway. It was Eric, who had gotten home early. He had seen the whole miserable event. He looked as white as a sheet.

"How long has it been, Vadie? How long have you been doing this?"

"Just today," I said, still wiping my eyes.

He sat down at the kitchen table with his head in his hands and then looked up at me.

"Don't fuck around with me, tell me the truth! This is serious. I feel so bad that I didn't even notice. What are we going to do? There are places that can help you; we need to tell your mom Vadie. How could I have missed this? You've been eating so much lately!"

"Well thanks a lot, you ass, but you don't understand. This is all so funny!" I couldn't stop laughing. "I was just trying to see if I could do it, that's all and I can't, so it's over. Don't worry about it! Now don't make me feel like I'm crazy or something." I tried to grab his waist and hug it all better but he stopped me.

"Vada, why do you try to make everything a joke? You are the mother of my children and I'm not going to let you do this to yourself." He went on and on. I have to admit I was trying not to laugh at that point, but it did make me feel good that he cared so much. As I looked into his brown eyes filled with fear and his lip shaking like it always does when he is nervous, something came over me. I knew I wasn't going to win this argument. I gave him a huge hug and gave in. I let him think that I needed help. I promised him that I would never do it again. I kept my end of the deal, but I know he never believed it.

Sitting here now in this group I would never admit that. I'll keep that information to myself. As far as everyone knows, I have an eating disorder. So that's what I will let them believe.

March 4th

The morning sun peeks in the window and after my breakfast of medication and oatmeal, I decide I am going to try out the spa. How incredibly wonderful! I saw this in the brochure and it looked like a resort spa. I can't wait to check it out for myself.

I throw on some lime green French terry pants, a little white tank top, and my flip flops and follow the signs to "Spa Therapy." I know they pointed me in the direction during my orientation, but I was too overwhelmed at the moment to pay any attention. After winding through hallways and following arrows, I see the blue sign with white letters, "Welcome to New Outlook Spa Therapy." I pull the door open and the smell of chlorine and lavender hit my nose. I have a nose like a basset hound, so I'm surprised I couldn't find this place by the scent alone.

I see a friendly-looking woman with curly blonde hair sitting at a desk. There are curved hallways that wrap around each way from where she is sitting. I wonder where those lead. She looks up at me and smiles. She asks me to sign in on the sheet. I see a list of names with check marks by them, and I sign my name at the bottom. She reads my name and looks up at me.

"Just one moment," she says sweetly. "You can have a seat if you like."

I take a seat on a bench with some magazines and I feel like I am getting ready to get my hair done at the salon and just waiting my turn. I must admit, this place looks really freaking nice. It's so calming. The floors are a rich dark hardwood and the walls are gray with white accent pieces. I start flipping through a random beauty mag, when Miss Front Desk looks up and says, "Vada Bower?"

Hmm...being as though I am the only person in the waiting area and I have such a common name, I'm sure it's necessary to use my first and last name because there must be at least a hundred "Vada's" here. What a douche. I stand up and walk to the desk.

"That's me," I say. (No shit) I would really like to ask her if she was looking for Vada Nicole Bower, or Vada Suzanne Bower, because if it was the Vada Suzanne, I would sit back down and wait for my turn. What an idiot.

"Well, Mrs. Bower, let me tell you about our services available to you today. You are what the center classifies as a Level 3. It's just the way we assess the risk level for our patients and what the hospital feels is safe for each individual."

She hands me a list of "spa services." I look over the list and my options are limited to meditation therapy, massage therapy, and aromatherapy. Well, what the hell? I could use a massage. I guess I'll take that. I realize that there are steam rooms and hot tubs here because I can smell them. Clearly, a Level 3 means they think I may drown myself. Fuckers. Well, it's fine. I don't much care for shared hot tubs. They are all probably full of fluidy infection anyway.

"We actually have a massage therapist available in ten minutes if you'd like to wait," says Miss Front Desk.

"Sure." I smile. "I'd be glad to."

I go and take a seat and pick up my magazine where I left off. My relaxing read about "Spring's Top Trends in Lip Color" is interrupted. I start to hear what I can only describe as a thudding sound and it is growing louder. It sounds like Big Foot is stomping through thick brush in the forest. It's coming from the winding hall down the left. I recognize the heavy breathing and I immediately know who it is. The sight that hits me first is a quite large royal blue one-piece swimsuit with a white daisy on the front. The wet stringy hair is clinging to her head in all directions and her toenails are a fungal yellow. Let's be clear here, they are not polished. She throws a white towel around her neck and stops dead in her tracks and we lock eyes. It's Bath Salts Mary, my roommate. I want to look away, but I can't. Through her skin-tight bathing suit, I notice her lowly hanging nipples are each pointed outward. One's looking southeast and one is looking southwest. There are long strands of hair hanging out the crotch of her swimsuit. Someone needs to prune that bush. What a creature. She is still staring at me. I look down at my magazine. But she does not move. I look back up. She is still staring.

"Mary, how was your hot tub experience this morning?" asks Miss Front Desk.

Mary finally looks away and turns her eyes towards Miss Front Desk. Why does Bath Salts Mary get to be called by her first name and why is she deemed safe enough for the hot tub? I'm kind of pissed now.

"It was nice. The jets felt good on my genitals," she says quietly and then looks back at me. I can feel myself about to gag. Mary turns towards me, like her bloodshot eyes are hungry for flesh.

I stand up. "Cancel me! I don't feel good!" I say, and I run down the hall and out to the Social Room with the big T.V. So much for the fucking spa! I'll never go back, and I have got to get my own room!

A Session about my Internal Dialogue...well...kind of...

Dr. Lipton, one of my two assigned therapists, pulls out a printed copy of one of my blog posts. He reads it out loud:

<u>*Doing the Mom Thing*</u>

Ladies, isn't it fun going to the grocery store?

I took my three boys to the grocery store this morning as we were in need of diapers and other grocery items. I would have rather stuck a pencil in my eyeball and set the end on fire, but I had to get it over with. As usual, the kids were really hyper and I had to be on them the whole time to stay with me. Jordan hates sitting a cart, but he has no choice. I forced him in and clipped the belt. I'm sure it looked similar to how someone would look putting a feral cat into a kennel. A family's got to eat and the food must be bought, so I had to do it. After filling my cart with milk and bread and meals for the week, I picked up some laundry detergent, the last thing on my list, and went to check out. There were only three lines open. I noticed that my shoes were slipping on something as I walked. Much to my dismay, the detergent lid had cracked and was spilled in a trail all over the floor. At this moment, a sweet faced Hispanic girl, who I would guess to be around seven or eight came up to let me know what had happened. Instead of saying "thank you" I looked right at her sweet face and said, "Oh motherfucker!" Seriously, why would I say that to a child? It just slipped out. It was now my turn to place items on the belt. I was trying to alert the cashier to what had happened, but he didn't seem to understand. My kids were starting to yell. I kept putting items on the belt. Jordan was screaming. I looked over and Max had found an open bag of goldfish crackers from the diaper bag, and had dumped it out on the floor and into the pile of Springfresh laundry detergent with sweat trappers and stain fighters. Ben was now begging for a candy bar.

By the way, what kind of complete idiot puts all that candy and crap by the register? It was obviously someone without kids or a brain. I realize it's the impulse buying scenario, but it is also just plain human decency not to put mothers through this. Does our happiness not mean anything to the corporations of this country? Please, continue to fill our minds with all this crap about living healthy and eating organic and raising our children to eat nothing but seaweed and vegetables. But while you are at it, please place one hundred different brands of candy and chips at every checkout line in America because you know that our kids will want it. I bought him a bag of M&M's. So sue me.

Anyway, the checker was the slowest person I have ever seen in my life. Seriously. As I moved forward to pay, I was stepping on the soapy goldfish. Crunch, crunch. I began loading bags into the cart. Ben had won the candy battle so he was quiet. Max had one leg out of the cart and I was holding Jordan while he was smacking the credit card swiper as hard as he could. I was afraid he was going to break the machine. I swiped the card, but the checker had forgotten some items. I swiped again thinking the sonofabitch was finally done, and yet there was still another item. Jordan was still beating the machine with all his might. Finally I swiped. I was done. I picked up my last sack of bread that now looked like a fucking pancake, completely smashed. The man then, only after we were finally done, asked me if I wanted to go pick out another laundry detergent. Are you fucking kidding me? He should have called someone to bring one up! I said no. I wanted to say, 'I'll go get another one, but only if you take off your pants, hold up your dick, and let me slam your balls in the cash drawer.' However, I simply smiled and carried on. I pushed the cart with one hand (Jordan was still in the other) and the weight of the cart crashed me right into the next checkout stand. Had there not been security cameras, I would have stripped butt naked and ran out screaming. I regained control. Max was still hollering and now riding standing up. I was carrying Jordan under one arm like a football. I bribed them out to my vehicle where I finally placed them in their seats and loaded up my purchases. Jordan was missing a shoe, yes that's right, a shoe. Well smack my ass and call me Gary. I decided to cross my fingers that the $30 shoe was somewhere in one of those bags because unless Colin Farrell was inside signing autographs with his dick, I was not going back in there...until next time...because I still needed laundry detergent.

Those were this mama's issues for today. Thanks for stopping by...and ladies...go to the store ALONE!

~V-Bow

Dr. Lipton sets the paper down on his desk and sits back in chair all nice and relaxed, clipboard in hand.

"That's quite an experience that day at the store," he says. His little wire-framed glasses sit on the tip of his pointy nose. He wants to read my blogs because he thinks it gives him insight into my mind...how profound!

"Yes it is," I say and nod politely. I'm in a recliner and the room is dim and cozy.

"I feel that your blogs have some sort of therapeutic value to you. Would you agree?"

"I think so."

"Why do you refer to yourself as V-Bow? Why not use your real name?"

"Well," I say, "I have three children and I am very involved in their lives. I don't want everyone thinking that I am some raging psycho with a foul mouth."

"So you are ashamed of what you have to say?" he asks.

Truthfully, well, kind of. I know I care too much about people thinking I am a bad mother, even though I know I take damn good care of my kids and it's not like I talk this way in front of them. But I look at him and say, "No, not ashamed. I just like to remain mysterious."

"Well, moving on, Vada, I have a few concerns about this post in particular. Do you mind if I ask you some questions?"

"Ask away Dr. Lipton. I'm an open book, or blog." I laugh.

"Well, I can see you had some strong opinions and emotions about taking your children to the grocery store, correct?"

This man is a fucking genius. No wonder he is a doctor.

"Yes, that is correct."

"I am wondering if this tension you were feeling could be avoided by applying some coping techniques. Slamming someone's testicles in a cash drawer is not a normal idea, Vada. I wonder if you could avoid this tension by learning to have better management of your children."

I'm trying to hold back...I'd like to ask him if he ever took his kids to the grocery store. I can almost guarantee that he hasn't. He's probably one of those chauvinistic jerk-offs who believes that's only the wife's job. I'd like to offer him the challenge. Right now. I could have Eric meet me with the kids at the grocery store and bring Dr. Lipton along and have him complete this chore without an ounce of stress. If he could make it through the store without thinking the word "fuck" at least one time, I'd give him a hand job. Sounds like a fair shake to me (pun intended). I'd like to see him do it. I'd also like to see peace in the Middle East, but some shit just doesn't happen. I hold back and let him talk.

"Tell me honestly Vada. Why so much foul language? Why do you feel the need to curse? Why do you feel so angry?"

I wish I could tell the truth and say I curse and have tension because my internal dialogue sounds just like Sam Kinison. I do not curse in front of my children, except for that one slip-up in the grocery store. The worst thing I may say is poop or darn it. That's why I do it on the inside or in my blog. That day in the store I really wanted to throw bananas at the checker's face and tell him to get a job down at the snail store because it was more his pace. But since I couldn't say or do those things, I wrote them down. Isn't that more socially acceptable than freaking out in public? I personally believe that every person has a little crazy in them. I believe that if we all said what we really thought our lives would turn out like a bad night of drinking. Everyone would cry and fight and then feel like shit the next day. So we don't. We smile and act polite. Some of us can hide it better than others.

"Well, I guess it's just anger, Dr. Lipton. I have so much anger built up inside of me. I have a lot of issues with my childhood and my life and it's all just too much." My words turn to soft cries. "I was left at a grocery store one day when I was seven. My parents were busy arguing about where my dad had been the night before. I wandered around to get away from them. I was just going to pick out some cereal, and when I tried to find them they were gone. They'd checked out and got all the way home before they realized I'd been left behind. I have always felt like I'm so easily forgettable. Can you imagine being a helpless child feeling like your parents had just forgotten you? I felt abandoned and scared. I can't even go down the cereal aisle! My kids don't even get to eat cereal, Dr. Lipton! It's all because of that incident when I was a child that I have a hard time even walking in to a grocery store."

There it was…verbal diarrhea, smoke, lies, and fairly good ones at that. I can't believe what I just said. Although my parents did have issues, this never happened. They got divorced like many people. I saw my dad once a week and things were civil. I sure as hell had never been left in a grocery store, or any other store for that matter. If anything, I was glad they got divorced and didn't put us through hell by staying together. The only reason I have a hard time going into a grocery store is because my children usually act like animals. Besides, they do eat cereal...a lot.

"Vada, I feel we have hit on a very important subject matter here and I want to hear more. Right now though, I think you should go back to your room and take a nap. Do you have any visitors coming this afternoon?"

"Yes," I said, "my best friend."

"Very good then. Get some rest before she arrives."

Hells yes I will get some rest. Thank you Dr. L. I'm going to follow doctor's orders and go off to shut my eyes. I haven't had an actual nap since recovering from my c-section with Jordan. I trot with joy down the hall and find my door shut. I carefully open it as not to disturb Bath Salts Mary, but I find she's not here. Hopefully she's off getting electric shock treatment; if not that, then maybe at least a good wax. I curl up into bed and set an alarm for three. That should give me a good three hours and I don't want to miss a minute of it.

Out of the corner of my eye I spot a blue piece of paper on the floor. It's a note:

Vada-
I'm on to you. Meet me in the Social Room at 9:00 p.m.
        ~Jessalyn

Oh crap. What the hell does she mean she's on to me? Oh well, this girl is not going to ruin my siesta. She's probably just one of those bullies like they have in the prisons and she wants to make me her bitch. I'm not scared. I could snap her wrists in two just by flicking them. Besides, I'm past the point of giving a damn. I shut my eyes tight and the anxiety medicine that Dr. Lipton prescribed me fills my dreams with little pink sheep.

Sabrina the Bestie

The alarm wakes me and I immediately look around for my kids, thinking we are late for school. I see the white sheets and remember where I am. Although the chill pill is good, it leaves me groggy. I shake it off and try to make sense of my hair and face before my friend Sabrina arrives. I slip on my flip-flops, a white t-shirt with a big red heart on it, and a pair of gray baggy boyfriend sweats. I go in and find what make-up they let me keep and dab some concealer under my eyes. I swipe on a quick coat of mascara to look more awake. It's amazing what mascara can do. A dab of cherry vanilla gloss and my shoulder length brown hair in a high pony and I'm good. Not that I have to look good for Sabrina, but I don't want to just totally let myself go. I mean my outfit is bad enough. I can at least touch up my face.

Katelyn comes in and tells me it's time for my visitor. I start to wonder about that note from Jessalyn. What in the world could she want? Maybe she's wanting to bribe me, but for what? Maybe she wants to scare me or something, although she didn't seem like the kind of person who would cause trouble. Who knows? But I can't shake this feeling that something is wrong. I walk in and see Sabrina sitting there waiting with a box of something. She is wearing a cute orange and gray color block shirt and jean capris. Her naturally blonde hair is in a loose knot behind her head.

Sabrina is the kind of friend who would literally pull an I.V. out of her arm if she was in the hospital to come help you change a tire. I don't worry about her knowing I am in here. She is also going to help keep an eye on my boys and I very much appreciate that. I'm glad she's here.

"Go home and change and put on something ugly and then come back and see me," I say as we hug hello.

"Whatever. You look fine," she says.

"Well, for the love of God, you don't walk in to the nuthouse looking all cute. Why don't you make us feel even worse about ourselves!" We both laugh and Sabrina grabs my arm.

"What?" I ask.

"What the hell are you doing here?" She looks at me trying to be serious.

"Sabrina, come on. I always told you I was going to end up here one day."

"I know, but I thought you were kidding...as in funny kidding."

"Sabrina, look at my eyes...what do you think?"

She looks back at me and I know she gets it. Sabrina has known me for thirteen years. We've been through everything together and she is literally like my soul sister. I know she is slightly concerned as she always is for me, but her smile tells me she understands. She asks me if we can take a walk and I nod. We walk out to a trail that runs throughout the property. It's peaceful and pretty. I think that's part of the "help." This is not your average mental institution. This is the cream of the crop, one of those nuthouses you see commercials for on television. There are fountains. There is an art studio. There is even a tennis court, although I don't play. The accommodations are very hotelesque. I'm able to get "luxury help" because I have really good private insurance and my mother received a settlement after her "accident."

A few years back, my mother was in a big department store when a wooden palette filled with paint cans landed on her leg. After being taken to the hospital where they found she'd suffered a broken femur and ankle, she got a nasty infection and they had to amputate her two little piggies; the one that didn't have roast beef and the one that wee wee'd all the way home. She recovered after a few months and some physical therapy. Although she looks ridiculous in flip-flops, she turned out okay. She did get a huge settlement. The rest of the family calls it an accident; she calls it "taking one for the team." So she helps out financially whenever she can, like paying for the kids' sports and things. Thank you, Mama. God rest her toes.

We reach a bench on the trail and have a seat. Sabrina opens up a box that looks like it came from a bakery. There's got to be a lot of calories in there.

"Did you bring cupcakes?" I ask. "How did they let you in here with those?"

"No, I brought brownies. And...I have my ways. Besides, I think the security guys want me."

"They probably do," I say, taking a brownie. "You know I'm going to throw this up right?"

"Shut up Vadie. Don't even joke about that."

I take a bite of this brownie all covered in powdered sugar and I am immediately taken back to high school. Sabrina brought me pot brownies. Holy crap. Should I eat this? Oh yes, I should. But what if I get caught? I guess they can treat me for that while I'm here. It's kind of funny actually. They can just add it to the list.

"I seriously can't believe you did this!" I tell her.

"That's what friends are for. Besides, I thought you might need to relax a little bit."

She puts the lid back on the box leaving at least five more brownies uneaten. We sit and eat our delicious and illegal brownies and talk about my kids and about her job and she doesn't ask too many questions. I do tell her about my roommate and for some reason she finds it quite funny. Sabrina doesn't have any kids, but she and I are friends with people whose kids go to my kids' school. She tells me she's talked to some of the people in our social circle. She swears she hasn't told a soul where I am. I believe her. I would die if anyone found out. You know how fast word gets around. What will the PTA say for crying out loud! I mean, people think I have it all together. From the outside looking in, I really do. It's just on the inside that I'm totally fucked up. Things start to get a little blurry and I stop and try to maintain my composure. The high suddenly creeps up and after chatting for a bit, we are definitely baked. I purposely bite my lip and narrow my eyebrows. I grab a hold of her hand and squeeze. I have something I want to tell her, and now is the perfect time.

"Sabrina, I have to tell you something, something serious."

"Okay girl, I'm here for you. What is it?"

"Well, I've wanted to tell you something for a long time now and I don't know how to say it."

"Vadie, what are you talking about? You can tell me anything right? So just shut up and tell me or I'm going to kick your ass."

"Alright, but you can't tell anyone okay? Especially Eric."

"Okay, now you're scaring me. I promise it's our secret."

"Alright then, you know how I've always had these big dreams about becoming famous someday?"

"No."

"Don't you remember me always telling you I had talents that no one knew about?"

Sabrina almost looks ashamed. She has no idea what I'm talking about. "No, I'm sorry, Vada, maybe you need to remind me because I seriously have no clue what you mean."

"Well, I thought I told you I wanted to be a rapper."

"Like a candy wrapper or a gift wrapper?"

"No, like a rapper-rapper. I want to be the first stay-at-home mom rapper to make it big in the industry."

Sabrina looks at me as if I'm losing it. She doesn't say a word.

I stand up and start spewing out lyrics that are coming from nowhere...

"Pulling up to the curb in my grey mini-van
Dropping kids at school, 'bout to get my errands ran
Had too many kids like the rest of the sluts
Now I'm in the looney bin 'cause they made me go nuts
My friend came to see me and we're getting kinda blazed
These brownies in my belly got me feeling kind of dazed
Next time she comes, she's gonna bring me mace
'Cause that Bath Salts Mary's bout to eat my fucking face
What time is it? It's time for meds!
So take some pills, get to your beds

What time is it? It's time for meds!
'Cause all us crazy bitches be sick in our heads"

I am dancing around like a complete fool and even do the cross my
arms pose. Sabrina starts beat boxing like this is completely normal.
Neither of us is cracking a smile. It's like we do this all the time, every day.
She is as terrible at beat boxing as I am at rapping. We both start
hysterically laughing even though it's not that funny. We can't stop. Tears
are rolling out of my eyes and Sabrina gets stuck on a laugh and starts
coughing, which makes us laugh even harder because she literally sounds
like she's dying. I start slapping her back really hard like I'm going to help
her get a chicken bone out of her throat and through her laughing and
coughing she yells,

"Quit fucking hitting me!"

This only make us laugh more because it dawns on us that I'm
practically trying to give her the Heimlich when she's not choking on
anything other than her own saliva. We are now both rolling on the ground.
I, for some reason, think it's funny to pretend like I am humping her from
behind since we landed in such an awkward position. We are rolling in
laughter. It's immature and so high school, but so funny at the moment.
When I look up, I see Nurse Katelyn staring at us with her arms crossed.

"Hello ladies!" she says. We stand up and quit laughing.

"Umm…Hi Katelyn. I have brownies," I say. Why the hell did I say
that? What an idiot. Sabrina looks at me in horror. I know my face is stuck
and I can't mutter another word. Katelyn says nothing.

"Well, I have to go!" Sabrina says. "Will you walk me out?"

"Shall I walk her to back to the visitors' quarters on this fine spring
day?" I ask Katelyn. Only I speak in an English accent. Okay, I seriously
need duct tape for my stupid mouth. I just need to stop talking.

Katelyn looks at me like she herself is in shock. "I guess so…I was trying to find you. We need to talk, so come to the nurse's station when you are finished." She looks at Sabrina, "Hi there, by the way."

"Greetings!" says Sabrina and she waves.

Katelyn turns and walks the trail back toward the building.

"Greetings?" I ask. "Did you really just say 'greetings' to someone? What are you, a fucking Christmas card?"

"Shut up, Vada. I'm so stoned. I can't take it. I was put on the spot! Don't make fun of me. You just had an English accent. What the hell was that all about?"

I take her by the arm and say, "Well, my little lawbreaker, let's get you out of here before they admit you too." I'm back to talking like an American. We are both still giggling like a couple of stoned teenage boys. We give a huge sigh of relief and let Katelyn get some steps ahead of us before we get it together enough to walk back. The afternoon sun is getting warmer and I think of my kids out playing. Guilt again stabs me in the gut. Closer to the building, there are other nut jobs out talking with visitors. There is even a yoga class going on. Hmm…I may have to try that.

We get to the back to the visitors' room with the big double doors. I briefly think about leaving. I could leave, couldn't I? I guess I haven't really thought about that. Am I legally bound to this place? Could I sign myself out if I wanted to? If I just walked out, would men in white scrubs come and hold me down while I thrashed and kicked and screamed? Would they inject me with a needle full of meds and tie me to a gurney while I piss myself and spit at them and shout obscenities? The whole dramatic scene plays out in my head and I laugh out loud. So does Sabrina, although I don't know what the hell she's laughing at. She hugs me tight and we say our goodbyes. She promises to go by the house tomorrow and check on the kids and she promises to give Eric a blow job while she's there. I say thank you until I realize what she said and we both laugh. I watch her leave and tell myself to screw the escape plan. I should at least try the yoga first.

The Smudge

I am starving and ready to eat a pregnant hippo, but I know I have to find Katelyn. I'm thankful that I'm starting to come down from the brownies. I really actually like Katelyn and don't want to piss her off. I don't plan on being here long, but I'd like to be on good terms if possible. The other nurses are so stuffy and dull. There is one named Wanda who doesn't smile and one named Gerri who has had so much plastic surgery I can't tell if she smiles or not. There are others but I really don't know any of them yet. I don't look long and I spot Katelyn before I even get to the nurse's station. She walks quickly over to me, pulls my arm, and jerks me into a room. It looks like an employee break room. There is a fridge, a table with folding chairs, and a schedule drawn up on a dry erase board. Luckily, there is no one else in here.

"I got you a private room," she says to my complete surprise.

"You mean away from Bath Salts Mary?"

"What? Who is...? Oh. Whatever. Anyways, we have an open room and I saw your request. But after what I just saw I guess it's safer for you to be in a single room. Many of our patients don't want to be humped."

"Oh, uh...sorry about that. We were just being stupid...and I..."

"Look, it's fine. But try not to get me fired, okay? I need this job and you are my responsibility." She stares at me and takes a deep breath. "Look okay, I just found out my boyfriend has been cheating on me and I need to get a place of my own. He's blown every dime I had in savings and ran up my credit cards buying big screens and video games, a new computer, a tablet, a new phone, and even some new golf clubs. That loser doesn't even golf. Now I'm flat broke. Hell, I'm worse than flat broke, I'm in debt. I'm staying in a hotel until I can get a place."

And there it is…a smudge. Her make-up is real. Tears fill her eyes and before I know it, she's hugging me. I'm not sure what to do, but I hug her back and she starts to sob. No wonder she looked like she was faking it here, this chick is a damned mess. She pulls me away and looks at me seriously.

"I need this job, so don't get me fired. Just be good."

"I'm so sorry!" I say honestly.

"Now get out of here and don't tell anyone what I told you. Your new room is 109 and you can move when you are ready." I look at her and she wipes all traces of her tears away, looking perfect once again.

I thank her and turn to open the door to leave.

"Wait Vada," she says. "I hope you cleaned up your mess."

Oh shit! I forgot to get rid of the brownies!

I am so hungry I could literally eat the silicon out of my boob. Is silicon toxic? Who knows...anyway they are both filled with it. I got a boob job after I quit nursing Jordan. I nursed all my kids for six months each and it was lovely, but when it was over I decided to shut down this baby bakery. I felt so bad about myself going from a C-cup to a DD-cup to a B-cup. Not to mention how sad my boobs were. My lady lumps looked depressed and really needed some perking up. Thanks to a little surgery and a lot of money, they are happy now. Happy and full and looking up at me like we are friends that had a falling out and now that we have made up, our relationship is stronger than ever. That is the one thing I have done for myself in six years that was totally selfish, but I am glad I did it and I'd do it again. Eric seems to enjoy the investment and I consider them to be a gift to both of us, so see, I guess it wasn't totally selfish.

It is seven o'clock, dinner time, but I know I need to find the box of brownies. I have so much to do. I need to move out of my room, find pot brownies, eat dinner for the love of all that is glorious, and I know there was something else, but I can't remember what. I decide that finding the brownies is probably most important, so I hit the trail and find the bench where we were sitting. No box, no trace, not even a crumb. Fantastic! Either there are some really high ducks flying around here or security found this and I will be arrested and have a mug shot. Maybe I can put my mug shot on Facebook! This is really great. Maybe I can FaceTime my kids' teachers from my prison cell for conferences. Bloody hell!

I start walking back and tell myself not to freak out. No one will know it was mine—until security finds the tape of Sabrina bringing it in. Okay, this is crazy talk. I need to chill the hell out. There is nothing I can do about it now and I'll just have to see if anything comes of it. I am going to really be crazy if I don't quit this paranoia shit that is burning like a wildfire through my head.

I choose to have dinner in the commissary. They give you a choice here to eat in your room or you can join the land of the living and eat in the group. It's considered a breakthrough if you eat with the crazies. Well, give me an award, because I can't make the trip back to my room to wait for dinner to be delivered. I go and grab a tray and find a seat at a table with the most normal looking gals I can find, four of them. They are eating quietly. Dinner looks good actually. It is some sort of lemon chicken pasta with cream sauce and asparagus. I eat like a hog. I must look like a freak show eating like this. It's one of those dinners you need real silverware for instead of this plastic crap, but clearly we can't be trusted with real knives. I'm not a cutter, but I guarantee you there are plenty of chicks in here who have an extensive cutlery set at home and some beautiful scars to show for it. I fiddle with my luxurious plastic ware and shove my mouth full. I know I've got shit dripping from my mouth, but I just don't care. When in Rome...I am slightly embarrassed but am still high enough to continue stuffing my face.

At least here I can eat with two hands. At home I usually have to eat

48

while standing over the stove with Jordan on my hip. Typically, he is screaming as dinner time is the witching hour. He is always fussy around five thirty, which so conveniently coincides with the fact that Eric is usually late getting off work. By the time I get a handle on dinner, the other kids have raided the pantry for fruit snacks and crackers, and I let them because I am simply trying to get the fucking dinner made and placed on the fucking plates. By the time I have food actually on the fucking table and everyone in their fucking places, no one will fucking eat! It's at that point that I feel defeated and tell everyone they may leave the table and I start cleaning up. And I shit you not. I...shit...you...not...the second every dish is done, the second that every counter is wiped down, the floor is swept, and the mop is hung to dry...they are all hungry. No joke. And to put the cherry on top of this sweet deal, Eric will run for fast food because he doesn't like leftovers, even if they were cooked that same night. Why do I even try? I guess because it's the law that I must feed my kids. I am simply trying to be a law abiding citizen and no one appreciates it. So eating my dinner like a lion eats a zebra after a rigorous chase when I have the chance, is no skin off my back.

After I fill myself to a satisfactory level, I look up only to see Rita, the puke counselor staring at me from across the room. Her eyes look as if she is taking great pity on me. I can imagine she's thinking I'm going to get a second tray and then pray to the porcelain gods. I try to avoid eye contact because I surely don't want her to come and talk to me. I try and start a conversation with the girls at the table, but it seems they are in their own little worlds. I wonder if I am at a table full of schizophrenics and they all are hearing little voices in their heads. I try again anyway.

"I don't know about you ladies, but I am full-ull." I say, sounding kind of like a hillbilly.

Not a one of them says a word. Perhaps they are not schizophrenics. Perhaps I have found the table of mutes.

"Well, my name is Vada. How long have you all been here?" Why the hell do I sound like such a nerd?

The women at the table all stare blankly at each other and then they start laughing, but they won't look at me. What the hell? What is this, like high school or something? I'm not crazy enough to be in their click? Screw them! They are still laughing. I had no idea there was like "cool" tables here in the nuthouse. I feel embarrassed and stupid and I'd like to kick all of their asses. I want to crawl into a hole. I've never been laughed out of a table before and these mentally ill women are laughing at me. I hurry and get up. They are still laughing. I can even hear one of them slapping the table, as I speed walk to the bathroom. I just want to get away. I go in and lock myself in a stall. Tears start falling down my face. What have I done? I miss my kids. I miss Eric. I want to go home. I decide that after I walk out of this stall, I will go and switch my stuff to the other room and get a good night's sleep. I plan to call Eric in the morning and see what I can do to get out of here.

I regain my composure though my eyes are still red, and I open the stall door. BAM. It's marga-fucking Rita, standing there, staring at me. I would almost it rather be the cops here to arrest me for possession. Could this get any worse?

"Dear, it takes time." she says, and puts her hand on my shoulder. "We are all in this together. Don't be too hard on yourself. I would like to know what you're feeling."

I look up in to her eyes through her red glasses. She is actually emotional about this. Here we stand outside the stalls with a lingering aroma of asparagus-scented urine, from what the girls have eaten all night, mixed with a hint of bathroom funk. This moment is awkward and I wish someone would walk in the door and save me. I feel like I want to break her glasses. Just take them off her stubby nose and crack them in two. That's how I feel. However, I watch my mouth and play the game.

"Oh Rita, I just was so hungry."

"I know sweetie, I know. So am I, shhh…shhh….so am I."

And there it is…a hug. I just take it, whether I want it or not, like a new bride with a headache. It's just something that must be done and we are now hugging are hearts out in the bathroom. She starts swaying me this way and that and I don't know where to place my feet. I feel like I am at a junior high school dance. Do we circle while we sway? I am so uncomfortable!

"I want you to tell your therapist about this tomorrow in your session, okay Vada? If you need me to be there with you, I will. I…"

"No!" I say way too quickly. I pull back. "It's just that…I feel like this will be good for me to come clean on my own. I want to start taking accountability for my own actions. I need to do this to help me get better." What the hell am I saying? "But I am extremely tired tonight and just want to get to my room, okay?"

"Alright dear, should we pray together?" She tries to grab my hand.

I fake cough and cover my mouth to avoid any more of this intimacy.

"Already did…right after I barfed. Prayed it all better and the Lord is happy that I'm done with the puking and I can now go back to my room and settle in. So thanks, but already talked to God and I'm pretty sure he forgave me for doing the technicolor yawn in there, so I'm gonna go now. Thanks Rita. Thanks a bunch. You are really good at this."

Rita looks like I just grabbed her ass and she has no clue how to handle it. So I walk out the door and leave her there puzzled, figuring she may as well use the toilet while she's in there. She's probably got some hacking to do herself.

Room 109

I know I have to go to my old room and I hope that Bath Salts Mary

51

is already asleep or out chewing cud somewhere because I don't want to have a one-sided conversation about why I am leaving. I'm just going to get it over with. I walk in quietly and there she is. Oh God. Those eyes turn my way. "Hey Bath-I mean Mary, I don't know if they told you yet, but I've been moved down the hall. Sure will miss having you as a roommate. I just need to get my things."

Mary looks different for some reason. She has make-up on. Huh…who would have thought? She's no Miss America but she cleans up at least decently. I'd say she's at least about a two or a three. And I'll be darned, but she's got on lavender satin pajamas. Who the hell is she dressing up for? I keep grabbing things and throwing them into my duffle bag. I swipe my stuff from the bathroom, grab my boys' drawings, and am ready to head out.

"Well, good luck to you Mary," I say sweetly and smile. "I know we didn't become the greatest of friends and I am sure we both have issues that—."

"Not to be rude," she interrupts, "but I'm expecting someone and if you could just stop talking and leave then I would like that." Her blood shot eyes are piercing through my skin.

I stand frozen. Did she just talk, like in human words? Wait a minute. Did she just kick me out? Has she got a boyfriend coming in here? Oh…does she have a girlfriend coming in here? Well, I guess I should leave before she gets feisty. But that bitch has a lot of nerve and apparently needs to get her freak on. Gross. I just look away and walk out the door.

I head to room 109. Why does it have to be an odd number? It is eight thirty and I am tired and ready for my sleeping pill in my little white cup. I must say, however, that this room is ten times better. There is a queen size bed with a fluffy white comforter and two fluffy pillows. There is a private bathroom and a closet with low drawers, no hooks, probably so we can't hang ourselves. There is even a little table with two fabric-covered arm chairs with floral patterns. They are a pretty sage green, cream, and pale yellow. It's kind of bed and breakfast-ish, but I like it.

I get my jammies on, pink flannel pants and a wife-beater. It's not quite as sexy as Bath Salts Mary's seductive satin number, but the thought of what lies under that lavender fabric gives me a strep throat taste in my mouth. I start to feel a little better about my lame jammies. I don't unpack, as I am still planning to call Eric in the morning to come get me. I do hang up the pictures my boys drew for me, because they make me happy. I then, lie in this deliciously comfortable bed and let out a sigh of relief. That is, until my door knocks and in walks Katelyn, perfect looking Katelyn.

"Hey there, just checking on your room. I have your therapy schedule for tomorrow and I brought your p.m. meds. How are you feeling?"

"Wait a minute, how are *you* feeling?" I ask.

"I shouldn't have told you any of that. I apologize for having a moment earlier, but I needed to get it off my chest. I guess even the nurses here have meltdowns sometimes. I should be helping *you* get better so don't even think another thought about me, okay?"

"Well okay, but you know there *are* ways to get back at this guy."

"What do you...no...just forget it. I need to move on with my life. Plus, I have one more patient to see before the shift switch."

"What, you're leaving?"

"Vada, I'm the day nurse. You have a different nurse at night. Have you not even noticed?"

"I guess the sleeping pills must really work."

"Okay, I'll be back in the morning and I'm trying to get overtime, so I may be here more hours than I normally would. Good night...take those pills first before I go."

"Hmm…a sleeping pill and a pooping pill I am guessing?"

"They give those to everyone. Most prescription meds clog your tank." This strikes me as funny because I bet Katelyn doesn't poop. Perfect people don't poop, do they?

"Thanks Katelyn, and if you change your mind and want some help with this guy…you know where to find me. I'm really good at screwing people up. It's always been one of my personal strengths."

"Thanks Vada. I'll see you tomorrow."

Katelyn walks out, shutting the door behind her. The door is big and creaky and kind of appropriate for a place like this. I can only imagine the different kinds of women who've been here before me, who have slept in this bed. There are so many reasons people are here and all of them seem somewhat normal to me. Aren't we all a little OCD…a little anxious…a little depressed…a little manic…a little paranoid…a little addicted to something? Aren't we all a little unbalanced?

My deep thoughts are interrupted by a knock on the door. For the love of Haley's Comet, can't a girl get some rest around here? I open it a crack and it's that Jessalyn girl. It's after nine. I forgot. I knew there was something I forgot; those brownies messed with my memory. I nervously open the door all the way to let her in. She is just a tiny little thing. She looks like a model with blonde waist-length hair that was left to air dry and magically looks like it's made for the runway. Her skin is pale and her face is pretty, like in a natural way, not a false eyelash kind of way. She seems to be in her jammies too: striped boy shorts and a red lacey tank top that says Nighty Night. Well dammit! I'm back to feeling lame.

"You got my note right?" she asks. She is twirling a strand of blonde hair around her finger.

"Umm…yes. I'm sorry. It's been a really busy day and I just forgot."

54

"Whatever." She looks off to the side as if deliberately trying not to make eye contact.

Awkward silence....ugh...I hate awkward silence.

"Did you need something?" I ask.

"I'm on to you." she tells me. *Duh*? Like I didn't read the note, but what the hell is she talking about? I don't love this conversation we are having.

"Well...congratulations, I guess." I just want to go to sleep and I can already feel the sleeping pill making my eyes all blinky.

"I know you're not really bulimic. I'm calling your bullshit on that one. So what is it really? Are you a pathological liar? A sex addict? Do you hear voices? Oh...wait, I know. You have postpartum, severe postpartum! Am I right?" she is laughing, still twirling her hair.

I do not know what to tell her. Who the hell does this girl think she is? I don't have to tell her a damn thing.

"Why do you care? Why are you making it your business?" I ask her.

"Because I don't like to see people spit lies all over my group. A lot of us have *real* eating disorders. It's not fun, okay? It sucks, and whatever it is you are trying to cover up as an eating disorder, well it's not my problem and I don't want people involved in our group who don't belong."

I point my finger at her like she's going to get it. "Okay, little girl, you may not understand me and that's fine, but you don't know a thing about me so until you do, I suggest that you focus on yourself. I've got enough going on and really don't need your shit, okay? I've got three kids at home and I don't need another one here, so thank you very much. You can go now." Wow! I'm way more ballsy than I thought. Actually, I'm kind of a bitch. Who knew?

She looks at me like I've just slapped her. In my mind I'm all like, what now biotch! You best be headed back to your room! But the mother inside of me sees a little broken girl who just needs someone to be mad at. She lets go of her hair and looks down at the floor like she is about to cry.

I soften my voice and I feel like I'm dealing with one of my children. "Come here and sit down." I walk over to the chairs and pat one with my hand. "Let's try to start over, okay?"

I can't believe it but she actually does. I really hope she doesn't stay long because Mommy needs sleepy.

"Alright, I'm sorry if I was rude. It's just been so hard being here," she says. "I feel so exposed...and the things I have told these women here and the story you heard...about my grandfather...well..." she starts crying.

I hand her a box of tissues, "What?" I ask. "You don't have to talk about it if you don't want to."

"But I *do* want to talk about it. I want someone to know! Nobody outside of this building knows! Everybody thinks, 'Oh Jess just wants to be a model' and 'Jess is starving for attention.' That's what my family and friends think is wrong with me. They all think that I'm obsessed with my looks and the truth is I hate myself because when I look at my body it reminds me of what happened to it!"

This little lady is now crying and I find myself crying too. I did not sign up for this. I am not equipped to deal with this. I need to find a nurse. STAMP! or STAP! What the hell is the word they say when the medical people need something quick? I know it starts with an S! STAT! What am I supposed to do with this girl? Maybe I should just let her talk and not say anything. Maybe I should just run out of the room and hope she doesn't follow me. But I think she came to me for a reason. There must be a reason. Words come out of my mouth, but I am totally winging this one.

"So, you are telling me that you never told anyone what your grandfather did to you? How old were you? When did it finally stop? Is he still alive?"

I ask so many questions and get so many answers. Jessalyn goes on to tell me the details of when she was six years old her grand-pig violated her for the first time. He lived in their house with her mother and drunken father. He told her that if she told anyone, that they wouldn't believe her and that he'd hurt her even worse. How freaking scary would that be for a child? Her mother died of an intentional drug overdose in the middle of all of this, when she was only eight. Her father left after that, so she was left with this creep to raise her. Apparently, her aunt moved in to help, but supposedly never caught on to what was happening at night. How could she not know? This old prick sounds like a real winner. He tortured her with threats, and the abuse apparently went on for years until she got her period at the age of twelve. It seems that the pervert only preferred pre-pubescent children, because then it stopped.

"Everyone thinks he's a hero," she said. "He was in the military, a war hero. He is well-known around town and has always been active in the church. Still to this day, they all worship him. He's almost ninety years old, but he's as alive as ever. Every time I've been forced to see him, he gives me this look, this creepy look. It's like he's warning me...still to this day...not to tell."

All I can do is hug her and tell her how sorry I am. She thanks me for being a good listener and I tell her that I am here for her if she needs anything at all, so to come see me anytime. She even promises not to rat me out at puke group. I think I'm going to like this girl. I just wish I could help her.

Before she walks out my door, she turns and looks at me with a smile and says, "Oh Vada, by the way...those brownies were awesome."

Shocked, I say "*You* are the one that found those? What did you do with them?"

She says through her smile, "I saw your little blonde friend bring them in. Sorry Vada, but I kind of ate one. Even an anorexic chick like me can enjoy a pot brownie now and then...and didn't you know? The anxiety girls had a little dessert before dinner tonight. I thought it would be good for them to have a laugh and chill out. I think it worked, don't you?"

I look at her completely clueless.

"Couldn't you tell? You sat at the same dinner table with them. They were so stoned. It was hilarious! Well, Good night...and thanks Vada."

Well, lift up my hood and jiggle my parts...no wonder they were all laughing. What a day! I'm going straight to sleep and I am not letting myself think about anything. I will try *especially* hard not to think about what Bath Salts Mary is doing right now in my old room, but I'll bet it's sticky and naughty and has an odor.

March 5th

My quack schedule for the day is light and I am relieved. My morning meds arrive, an antidepressant and a benzo of some sort, in other words a crazy pill and a chill pill. Yes please! Katelyn is not back yet, so I get Gerri, the plastic face nurse this morning. I wonder if her face hurts. I wonder if she thinks fondly of her surgeon and the job he did. I watch her try to smile, at least I think that's what she is doing, and I see the skin on her bottom lip actually pulling apart. She's going to need some ChapStick for that because I think it cracked, may even be bleeding, but the wine-colored lipstick keeps it a mystery. Yikes! Her hair, which I am sure is gray underneath the golden dye, is a ponytail set high on her head. I can't quite tell if it's an extension or a clip-on ponytail, but I do believe that whatever it is, once belonged on the top of a horse's ass. It's definitely not human hair. But what the hell, she's doing her thing.

I eat waffles and yogurt in my room. I always eat breakfast in my room. The whole breakfast in bed thing is fascinating. You lay there, someone brings you food, you eat it, you leave it, and they clean it up. Brilliant! I get in a nice long hot shower. My therapy appointment is at nine o'clock, so I take my sweet time getting ready. I throw on a hoodie and my stretchy pants because according to the calendar and pains in my worn out uterus, my lady friend is coming to visit today. Woop-a-dee-dooh!

After finding out last night that the "mean girls" that I thought were laughing at me were really just baked, I decide to call Eric and check on the boys, but I don't hatch a plan to bust out. I might as well ride this thing out...at least a little longer. Eric says the boys are fine and they will visit soon. He reminds me how much he loves me and that he is so proud of me and can't wait for me to be home. I bet he's telling the truth because usually if I run out, even to the grocery store, he looks sweaty and anemic by the time I get back. I smooch kisses at my boys on speaker phone and tell them how much I love them and miss them. They tell me they are going to build me the coolest LEGO tower I've ever seen. Ben tells me that a girl in his class today told him that her mom is a dumb-ass. Although it kind of surprises me, I wonder what he told her about his mom. I can only imagine,

"Well, my mommy's in a mental institution and can kick your mommy's ass 'cause that bitch is crazy!" Oh, can you imagine? The boys think I am at the doctor to get some rest. They are so smart though, they probably aren't even buying this bullshit.

After my call, I decide to take a walk to ward off the cramps. As I am walking down the long hallway, I see the door open from my old room. It's probably Bath Salts Mary heading to yoga. I can't help but get a mental picture. I can imagine her eyeballs popping out and rolling on to her yoga mat while doing the downward dog and then the blood bath that would take place after she started ripping the flesh off the other participants and whipping their skin around in her jowls like a dog eating a pork butt. A tall woman leaves the room stepping quickly, like an invisible elf is walking behind her and jabbing a sharp stick up her ass. This is not Bath Salts Mary, this is someone else. I see a long blonde ponytail and navy blue pants with a white long-sleeved shirt, but I can't see the front. Whoever it is must have spent the night and whoever it is clearly has a sore bum. Who is this? I must know. I pick up the pace and try to catch up. I never see her face, but I do see which room she goes into. She quickly shuts the door behind her. Well, hell…somebody's got a little night-crawler around here. I'm not one for gossip, but curiosity may just kill this cat. Hmm…room 74. I'll remember that.

Suicide Risk

Another room filled with glee. There is soft music, a nice comfy couch, and a big fluffy pillow. The walls are a tranquil blue and Dr. Ames, my other designated therapist, is a stout little fella with at least four chins and droopy eyelids. He sure seems like a nice enough guy, but I don't care to get to know him. In fact, he seems too nice to be for real. Something is off about him. I just don't get a good feeling. I see a picture of him and his wife on his desk. Oh well, he must be at least somewhat normal. I'm sure I am just being paranoid.

My plan is to get this over with so I can get back to some quiet time.

His smile is literally from ear to ear and he welcomes me and offers me something to drink. I choose iced tea and he seems all excited that I accepted his offer. I'd rather have a vodka&7, but I don't think that's on the menu. He tells me to get comfortable and his smile fades only when I ask if the pillow case on the pillow is clean. He grabs a cup of ice from his mini-fridge and pours me some tea.

"I can assure you Mrs. Bower, may I call you Vada?" I nod. "I can assure you that it is clean. The staff always changes the pillowcases after each session. It says here in your chart that this type of thing may be a problem for you, is that correct?"

Well, if you think it's a problem for me that I don't want to get head lice or to touch some other person's drool…or hairs… or flakes of their dead skin cells, and that I don't want to put my head on a spot where some nasty person's snot may have gotten wiped on, then yes it's a problem for me.

"Umm…I was just checking. I'm a mother and laundry is part of my life," I say, trying to ease myself out of that topic.

"Alright, Miss Vada, today I want to jump right into this. Don't hold back. You are in a place of no judgments. I want you to think of this room as a box, okay? Try with me to imagine this room is a little box and you safely place your thoughts and secrets into this box. You can lock it up when you leave. Only you have the key. Are you imagining this, Miss Vada?"

What the hell is he rambling on about? What a silly little man.

"Yes, Dr. Ames. I totally get it."

"Good. Now remember, you hold the key, you turn the key, so open your box now."

Did he really just ask me to open my box? I want to burst out laughing. I try to be serious.

"It's open," I say, holding back a giggle, but in my mind I wonder what he'd do if I dropped my drawers and spread my legs. I wonder if he'd stop using this ridiculous metaphor, but who knows...maybe he's really a pervert and is thinking the same thing.

"Okay, I want to go back to the night when you were on the roof, do you recall that night, Miss Vada? It was the night you wanted things to end. I know this may be difficult, so take your time."

I'd like this to end right now so I can go watch *The Golden Girls* marathon in the T.V. room. I know what he is referring to and I knew this was going to come up at one point or another. I guess I better get this over with so I can get back to my rest and relaxation.

He starts reading from his clipboard, "The incident occurred this past winter, Christmas Eve. Your husband was very concerned about this. Tell me what led to you being up on the roof. What was going through your mind?"

"I just wanted the noise to stop. I had a headache. I just wanted to find some peace. That's all...some peace. Some quiet. Some calm."

He looks at me concerned and writes down some notes.

I think back... Christmas had been an absolute freak show. I was so stressed about how much money we were spending trying to buy gifts for what I felt like was a million people. I had the kids' Christmas parties at school, plus their programs to go to. I had my husband's company party where you have to look like one of the Real Housewives in order to step in the door. Let me tell you, being a stay-at-home mom at a company party is super fun. Not really. Everyone dresses like they are something special and everyone's got these big bad jobs and their stupid business jokes which make me want to lick a mousetrap every time I hear one. But it wasn't just the parties; it was actually Christmas...making the rounds to see all the family so that no one gets offended. I always have to cook crap that I don't even like, like casseroles. Just the word casserole makes think of dirty dishes. I'm always baking cookies and burning cookies. I have to explain to the family why everything I bring to Christmas dinner sucks, and it sucks even worse knowing my mother-in-law wishes I could feed her son better food. It stresses me out watching the kids open presents from relatives and then I cringe when they toss them to the side. At least they try to be polite sometimes. Max actually opened a little toy phone that would have been more age appropriate if he were a two year-old and he looked up with big sweet eyes at his great uncle and said, "I don't really like that, but thank you anyways." Of course I pretended not to hear and bolted my ass out of the room. It was Eric's side of the family, therefore I felt like he needed to smooth that over. Of course, I still stressed about it. Just the overwhelming feeling of too much to do with too little time, all while trying to teach the kids the real meaning of Christmas, and also making their Santa experience magical and memorable.

"Whenever you are ready, Vada. Remember your box."

Hahahahaha!

"Okay Dr. Ames, I remember being overwhelmed. There was just so much going on. I had some trouble getting the gifts together and making everything perfect. I wanted to make everything special for my kids, you know?"

I'm not going to tell Dr. Ames this, but I do remember. Christmas Eve after my little lovies finally fell asleep, I was putting together a race track with my eyes halfway open when I realized the 4 D batteries were not included. I remember my eyes burning with tears and I felt like getting a kitchen knife and stabbing the damn box. Why the fuck couldn't it say "batteries not included" in BIG letters on the box? They should be included anyway! I paid seventy-five bucks for this piece of shit plastic track and you want to tell me that I have to pay an additional ten bucks and leave the house in the middle of the night on Christmas Eve when its sixteen degrees and snowing outside! Why doesn't Santa Claus get off his big fat lazy ass and get them himself? I was so pissed and I am embarrassed to admit this, but I did smack it around a bit. I threw one of the cars and kicked the shit out of the empty box and then I laid down on the floor by the Christmas tree and cried. I cried and cried and cried. Eric came down to see if I needed any help. I bet he wishes he wouldn't have. I remember saying something along the lines of, "If you don't find a 24-hour store and come back with 4 D batteries and a large Diet Coke with extra ice and some Milk Duds in fifteen minutes, I will literally test out this motherfucking race track with my minivan." I think it was thirty minutes, but he made it happen. He also stayed up and helped me get everything else ready for Christmas morning. Unfortunately, it took me almost having a nervous breakdown to get any help.

"So you were feeling stressed and overwhelmed by the season, this is very common Miss Vada, go on..."

I wish he'd quit calling me Miss Vada, I'm not a damn preschool teacher!

"Okay, umm...I had some trouble getting the gifts ready and umm...my family came. My family is dysfunctional. They have a lot of problems and I guess I am just not very good at dealing with them."

I'm remembering what really happened on Christmas morning. My family always comes to watch the kids open presents. My mother always brings an insane amount of gifts for the kids. My mother is a sweet lady. She is one of those ladies who would literally give you the shirt off her back if you needed it. She has short gray hair, because she doesn't want to mess with coloring it even though she's only fifty-three. She wears glasses and is a cute little grandma. You can't help but like her even though she can be bossy at times. Her intentions are always good.

My father and my brother, Heath, showed up and they were at each other's throats. Heath and dad have a love-hate relationship. Heath still has issues with my parents getting divorced. He was always so sensitive. Although my parents have been divorced for many years, they too have a love-hate relationship. My dad walked in and grabbed the baby and I could see my mother's eyes dilate and focus and I knew she was pissed that he got to him first. It's always a competition.

My dad is kind of immature. Don't get me wrong, I love him with all my heart, but he's like a six year-old in a fifty-four year-old body. He is always telling jokes, which are quite funny actually. But, he is always getting into some kind of trouble. He's constantly trying to win sweepstakes and get on game shows. He's the kind of guy who will bet it all on red, literally. He loses money as fast as he makes it. I can't tell if he's a compulsive gambler or if he just really likes to play games. He always exceeds the limits at the casino, but you should see him at a state fair. The man will literally spend hundreds of dollars playing carnival games, like popping balloons with darts and bouncing frogs with a hammer and getting them to land on a lily pad. My kids love it because they come home with bags full of stuffed animals and bouncy balls. He's a kind-hearted man, but really, he is still a child.

Heath is five years older than me and divorced with no children. He's a good guy who loves weed by day and bourbon by night and needs to find a good gal who wants to marry a guy who loves weed by day and bourbon by night. His ex-wife was one of those patchouli oil chicks, very beautiful in a hippie kind of way. She always wore long skirts and tight shirts. She always had some new remarkable thing she had discovered, like a new hookah, or a piece of jewelry that could read your mind. They were a good couple, but quite honestly, I think they didn't work because Heath drank too much. The pot didn't bother her. She was always smiling, if you know what I mean. He hasn't done too badly though since the divorce. He started a moving company and him and my dad and two of his buddies bought some moving trucks. They actually run a pretty good business and it helps to keep them out of trouble. The only problem is that business and family don't always mix well, as they are slowly learning.

Heath and Dad were off whispering in the corner, probably something to do with money, and Mom came out and told them both to just leave and that they weren't going to ruin Christmas for everyone by telling secrets. It always starts off this way. I had to calm everyone down and convince everyone to stay. I was exhausted before I could even finish the greeting part!

"Dysfunctional can mean many things, Vada. Can you explain?"

"Well, Dr. Ames, I guess everyone has issues and I'm usually too involved in trying to sort out other people's lives than to focus on my own."

I lay there remembering how that day came and went and the baby cried and the kids laughed and then fought and everyone had too many cocktails. Except for me because I was too busy taking care of the kids and cleaning up. My mom helped a lot, of course, by wiping shit down and doing dishes, but then she started doing laundry. I remember telling her, "No no no...there is no laundry on Christmas. I'm not doing this today." She retorted by telling me, "I was just trying to help, but if you don't want my help then maybe I should just leave." That made me cry and then I joined her in folding clothes. After that was done, she came up and put her little arm around my shoulder and said, "Now, aren't you glad that's done?" But I wasn't glad. I wanted to go throw the laundry basket upside down in the snow. I wanted to do something other than chores on one freaking day of the year. So no, I was not glad. I was pissed. But I just smiled and thanked her and told her yes. Why is it that on holidays everyone else gets to relax and have a good time except for the moms? The men all go off and lay down because they are "so full" from the meal that they were just cooked and served. I swear one day I am going to make a mommy's only Christmas party and me and my mommy friends are ordering in and hiring a cleaning service (of men) to clean up after us. Men shouldn't even be invited to Christmas as far as I'm concerned. Once a guy turns eighteen, I say we just send them a card and wish them a Happy New Year.

"Well, Miss Vada, when we neglect ourselves it can lead to serious problems, which we may not realize until it's too late. Let's talk about the roof, shall we?"

"Dr. Ames, it was a moment of weakness. When I went up on the roof that night, I may have wanted to kill myself, but then I thought of all the reasons I needed to live, my children, my husband. I may have had suicidal thoughts, but almost dying that night has changed me forever. I cherish every day now. I'm in a new stage in my life and it's called living!" My pants are on fire from these lies. Jiminy Cricket needs to step in and tell me it is wrong, but he must be choking on the smoke.

"Vada, I can see you are getting emotional about this, let's lock up your box for the day and you can go and have some free time. I think you learned a lot that night about life and death and I'm confident that you are not at a high-risk for repeating that behavior. Here are some pamphlets and phone numbers should you ever find yourself back in that type of situation."

I take the junk mail, I lock my box, and I thank Dr. Ames. I quickly leave the room and scurry outside for a walk on the trail, remembering the true event of the roof. I toss the papers in the trash on my way outside.

That Christmas night amidst the chaos of the food and family, Eric pulled me aside and wanted to see me. I knew it was because he wanted to do our little gift exchange. I was excited because it was a moment that we could just spend together and talk. I had gotten him some new boots that I knew he would love. They were cowboy boots, but not the cheesy kind. The kind he could wear with jeans and a t-shirt and look perfectly himself. That is so his style. He's a scruffy but handsome guy. The kind of guy who doesn't know he's good looking.

He opened his gift and kissed me and smiled. It was a sweet moment and then my turn came. I opened a plastic bag, not a gift bag, a plastic bag. Inside I found a box with a blue phone in it. "I already had all of your contacts and everything switched," he said. "I thought you needed a new phone."

I stared blankly at the new blue phone. My contract was up for renewal and it dawned on me that this was the free phone that came with the plan. I didn't know what to say. I was going to go up this week and renew my contract. Was this really my gift, a free fucking phone? That's not a gift. It wasn't even wrapped. All it was really good for was that it saved me a trip to the store, which by the way, I would have liked because I really needed to get out for a minute! Oh hell...no. Please don't bother to wrap my free gift because I've only searched for, bought, and wrapped 100,000 goddam gifts for you and your freaking family, and the family we adopted, and even the mailman! I even wrapped the gift for your mom's fucking Jack Russell terrier!

I looked up at Eric and smiled, trying my best to hold back tears. "Thank you honey, that was so sweet." I wished him a Merry Christmas. He said Merry Christmas back. In his eyes, I was thrilled. In my eyes, I wanted to hurt him...not badly, just maybe chuck a phone at his mouth and possibly chip a tooth.

We went back to the ruckus which was our family Christmas. The house was loud and company kept stopping by. New video games were blaring and I felt like I had taken a hit of acid or eaten a mushroom and so many things were happening all around me and I had this blue fucking free phone in my hand. I went to Eric and told him I needed to get away for a minute, so to please keep an eye on the kids.

The truth is that after I excused myself, I went up to the master bathroom and sat on the lid-closed stall. Knock knock...it was Ben and he had to go *really* bad. Okay, I gave that room up. I went and sat in the rocking chair in the baby's room, but was found by my pregnant cousin who wanted to check out our crib. I went to the sub-basement, but my father-in-law found me when he came down to look for some tools we "must have borrowed and never returned, like usual." I could have gotten pissy, but we never return anything we borrow, so I can't fault the man for telling the truth. The smokers were in the garage, and since I hadn't had the opportunity to have an alcoholic beverage, I couldn't join them. I went and grabbed my coat out of the hall closet and walked out the back door. With all the windows, I knew someone would see me and want something.

"Where's your Kleenex, Vada? Do you have a dish I can put this in, Vada? Are there any clean cups left, Vada?" I wished they'd all just shut the hell up! Find it yourselves, you donkeys!! I just needed to find a place where no one could find me. And just like that I saw a ladder, like a Christmas angel placed it there from out of the sky. Actually, I think my neighbor must have left it out when hanging his Christmas lights. The roof! I was going to hide on the roof! I stepped through the crunching snow and stole the ladder as quietly as I could. I leaned it up against the house and just started climbing. The back yard looks down to a drop off, and it would be a pretty big fall so I was extremely careful. I made my way up and realized that it was more dangerous than I had originally thought. The snow sat on top of ice and I knew that with one wrong move, this could end up in a bad way. I stepped off the ladder while grabbing on to the point of the roof. I found a safe and quiet spot and took a deep cold breath of air. It was quiet. All I could hear was the wind. I was actually savoring the moment. I love Christmas, and my family, and most of all, my kids. But I needed a minute, and I thought no one would look for me up there. I didn't think about chores, my calendar, meals, or anything. I was just listening to the wind and having my moment. It was peace. It was exactly what I was looking for. I could almost hear the night wind singing that song to the little lamb. I said a prayer while I was up on that roof. I closed my eyes and realized how thankful I was for those little boys I had underneath me in that house. Despite the danger, the freezing cold air, my frostbitten fingers, and my runny nose, that roof was exactly where I wanted to be at that moment.

After about ten minutes and once my extremities were beginning to turn blue, I knew it was time to go back down and rejoin the family. I had recharged. I wasn't even thinking about the phone anymore. As I placed one foot on the ladder, I immediately slipped on the ice and the ladder went crashing to the ground. Motherfucker! Luckily, I was still in a good spot on the roof, but there was no way to get down.

I leaned over to look down, when I heard "Vada! Don't jump!" It was Eric. He scared the shit out of me and I lost my balance and slid. It had happened so fast, the next thing I knew I was hanging on the gutter by my knuckles. I couldn't speak or scream. I was so scared. My feet were dangling beneath me and my fingers were so numb I couldn't even tell if I was holding on tight.

"Vadie! I'm coming to get you. Hold on! Don't let go baby!" Eric was coming to save the day.

With the help of the stupid ladder and Eric's superhero actions, I was alive and now my husband actually thought I had planned to jump off the roof to my death on Christmas. Really? I mean really or not? Maybe I *was* crazy. I tried to convince him of the truth and he finally said he believed me, but I know deep down he thinks I was trying to do the swan dive of death. I let him add that to the list of Vadie's "concerning" behaviors. Oh well, at least he cared. I still can't help but think that if I would have died that night, I bet he would have wished he'd at least gotten me an upgraded phone.

An Idea

After my half-truthed therapy session, I go outdoors to the courtyard. It is a beautiful day out here today. The flowers are all blooming and I can smell the lilac bushes every time the breeze blows through. I see a brunette lady my age wearing jeans and a camouflage sweatshirt off in the distance talking to a nurse, and for the first time I think I am witnessing a psychotic episode. I've always wanted to see one of these, not because I think it's funny. I don't enjoy other people's pain, but I want to see and hear it, to compare it to my internal dialogue. Am I one of these? Do I have the potential to become one of these? I am curious. I nonchalantly pretend that I am just looking for some shade and I hunker down under the big weeping willow tree and pick at the grass.

The woman is hollering something that I can't make out. She looks like she is dodging invisible asteroids falling from the sky. The nurse is on her little walkie talkie thing and looks in a state of panic. The woman is now becoming louder and I can make out, "Nobody came! I sent out the invitations!" She is running in circles and throwing acorns. "Party

Poopers! Shitheads! I don't like clowns! There is no cake," she yells, "where's the cake, you fucknuts?" She belts this nurse in the face with an acorn. I've never seen anything like it in all my livelong days. Poor nurse, she got it right between the eyes. Two males and one female, all in scrubs, come running out and surround this poor lady. They take her slowly down to the ground and a short mustached man gives her a shot. She calms down. They get a stretcher and take her inside.

Well crap, it *is* like in the movies. I realize at this moment that I have tears in my eyes. This person is somebody's somebody. How sad they would have been to see her like this. I wonder what happened to that poor woman.

"Bet you're wondering what happened to that poor woman, huh?" It's Jessalyn and she walks up by me and sits down.

"Where did you come from and how do you know?"

"I came from my evaluation, and I know because you are a worrier."

"Well forgive me for caring. I may be a worrier, but you are famished."

We both start laughing, and it's strange that we are already at that point where we can laugh and make jokes about our problems. That's how I have always dealt with problems, I make jokes.

"You really wanna know about her?"

"Yeah, sure."

"Well, that my friend was psychosis. Her name is Lauren Sanders and from what I know about her, she thinks every day is her birthday. When her therapy team tells her it's not her birthday she tends to flip her shit. I haven't seen it this bad yet, but I can only imagine it will get worse. I sometimes don't think these people have a clue how to handle crazy people."

"That's so sad!" I say. "Why don't they just tell her happy birthday and get it over with?"

"I don't know their reasoning, but I think they are trying to get her to accept reality. I mean, I've seen her go through this every day since I've been here, not this bad, but she's always crying and telling people they forgot her birthday. For some reason, she calls everyone a shithead. I don't know why. She'll even call you a shithead if she likes you, so I don't think she's being rude on purpose."

As I watch this poor lady get hauled away, I can't help but think that this must be a miserable life. What's so special about birthdays anyways? For my birthday this year, I got a yeast infection. I also had two kids throwing up with stomach flu and I got a bouquet of grocery store flowers with the eight dollar price tag still on it. Eric brought it home for me while picking up medicine for the kids. Happy fucking birthday to me! I almost sent him back to the store to exchange the flowers for a cactus so I could take my underwear off and sit on it. What a fun day. What a reason to celebrate!

"Well, everyone here has a story, ya know? Someday I will find out yours." Jessalyn sits twirling her hair.

Changing the subject I say, "So Jessalyn, how was your evaluation? Are you gonna be leaving soon?"

"I saw whatcha just did there, and I'm gonna let it slide this time, but next time you are gonna answer some of my damn questions. And yes, it looks like I may be going home soon. I gained six pounds and Rita is going to continue to sponsor me once I'm home."

"That's great, lady!" I say. "Where is home?"

Her hair is blowing in the wind and it's obvious that this girl is model material. She looks like she's doing a photo shoot or something. If I let my hair blow in the wind it would probably end up flat across my head and land in my mouth and I'd be picking it out of my teeth. She looks up at me and says, "I don't know yet, maybe a friend's place for a while. If I'm lucky I can make it to my grandfather's ninetieth birthday party on Friday."

"Are you serious? He's really having a birthday party? With like cake and ice cream? It's not fair that he gets a birthday party and that Lauren lady doesn't," I say, and I'm only *kind of* joking.

"Well, the rest of the family worships him. I'm telling you the truth. They've been calling here leaving me messages to tell me how important it is that I be there, it may be the last birthday he will ever have. Apparently, the old man is having some health problems. I say, see ya later sucka! That's all. Enjoy hell, you old nasty bastard! There's no way I am going to that party and it's going to piss a lot of my family off, but I don't care. Maybe I should just get online and send him a little doll with pigtails all wrapped up in a bow and he can go home and have his way with it, the pervert." Jessalyn looks over at me expecting me to laugh. "Hey. What? Why are you looking at me like that?"

"Jessalyn, I have an idea."

Blood and Charts

It is three fifteen. I am sitting in Dr. Lipton's office, and he is late. I am having a little eyeball foreplay with my chart and I wonder if he'll be late enough where I can take a looksy before he gets in. Maybe it's the anxiety meds, but I'm just more carefree than I usually am, so I waltz over to his desk and pick up the file. There are the words...the diagnosis: bipolar with hyper-sexuality. What the...? I am not a sex addict. My eyes roam the chart until I realize the name on the top is not mine. It belongs to someone named Mary Weaverton, age thirty-nine. Holy hell, it's Mary, as in Bath Salts Mary. The door creaks. I drop the chart and pretend like I am coughing.

"Are you alright, Vada?" Dr. Lipton walks over to me quickly.

"Just need water," I say still coughing.

Dr. Lipton walks out. I can't believe what I have just read. I have a problem; to take the chart or not to take the chart? That is the question. The angel on the right side of my shoulder is giving me a warning glare, but the devil on the left is bent over and twerking. Before I have time to think, I see shadows of footsteps under the office door and I pick up the chart, fold it, and slip it down the back of my pants. The door opens and in walks Dr. Lipton. This was a bad choice. The corner of the folder is digging into my left ass cheek and it's ridiculously uncomfortable.

"Here is your water."

"Thank you!" I say, acting like I am still recovering.

"Have you come down with something Vada?"

"I think I have something in my throat. I've always had acid reflux. Who knows...(cough) I have had a cough on and off for a while now." (lie)

"Well if you do suspect an illness let your nurse know, there's meds for that." He writes something down on his clipboard.

Well, you don't say, Dr. Oz? There is? There's meds for stealing people's personal medical files so that I can read them for my own selfish purposes? What a cutting edge facility!

"I'd like to start with a blog post of yours that I read. I have some questions for you about some things that concern me Vada. How is that?"

"If that's what you feel is necessary," I reply sweetly, trying to squirm my butt around to avoid paper cuts. At least I'm in the recliner. Getting up will be the tricky part.

"Okay then, let's begin with your blog post from early January."

He pulls out a copy and begins reading...

Doing the Mom Thing

Hello fellow mamas,

Today, I had the world's most difficult shower. Let me begin by saying my kids sleep with me. I know, right? Shoot me in the face, right between the eyes. I should be laid to rest because I break the rules and let them sleep in my bed sometimes. But there are literally days when I am so tired that I would let them sleep in my dresser drawers or in my bed while *I* sleep in my dresser drawers as long as they will sleep. What an out of control mother I am!

Now that we've got that part out of the way, my freaking neck hurt because I usually sleep with my head hanging off the bed. Also hanging off the bed is typically my left boob, left arm, and left leg. It's not the most comfortable position. Well, waking up and cracking my neck is a routine for me now, and then I get a shower...if I am lucky, very lucky. I tried to run the water as hot as possible so that it would hit my neck and loosen it up. The boys were all still asleep, so it was my fucky-lucky day, or so I thought. The hubs had already left for the airport on a business trip, so it was just me and my hatchlings at home. I got the steamy water running when I heard a cry...I turned it off...silence. It was my imagination. I turned it back on and hopped in letting the water work its magic. I got my shampoo in a nice rich lather and BAM...a cry. Now this is a tough situation for me. I have let the baby cry before and found his leg stuck in his crib bars, so I don't like to chance it. I turned off the water with sudsy hair, grabbed a towel, and scurried to check the video monitor. He was sound asleep. I realized that I was hearing phantom cries. My mind was screwing with me. Water on...heat on my neck, rinsing my hair. Conditioner...and then it was time to scrub the pink parts. BAM...cry...loud cry. I thought it was just a phantom cry, so I continued to scrub a dub and

75

get all ph-balanced and fresh. But this cry...it didn't stop. I had not yet rinsed the conditioner. I turned off the water and threw on a towel and put my soggy hair in a clip. I checked the monitor and the baby was still asleep...but I still heard a cry. I ran down the stairs to find Max, my five-year-old wailing in the living room. I asked him what was wrong and he said there was someone at the door, but he knew he wasn't allowed to open it. I glanced over at the front door which has panel windows on both sides. I've been too cheap to buy window treatments for them, so anyone can see in. To my horror, there was a pretty young male thing at my door with green eyes, blonde hair, and a clipboard. He could see me just as well as I could see him. Mind you, I was in a towel with conditioner caked in my hair. I inched my body behind the door as much as possible and tried to wave him off like "it's not a good time." He just wouldn't leave. What the hell is wrong with this delectable-looking brut of a man? Couldn't he see that I wasn't decent? I hid behind the door and barely cracked it open and told him politely, I didn't want to buy anything. "Ma'am, I'm so sorry to bother you, but this is certified mail and I need you to sign for it." What the fuck is wrong with this asshole? Why is he calling me ma'am. Am I that old? I discreetly grabbed the clipboard and did my best to sign it behind the door where he couldn't see me. I was actually pulling this off pretty well. I passed the clipboard through the cracked door and he handed me an envelope. I realized this situation was thankfully over until Max yelled out, "Mommy...I can see hair on your girl butt, the one in the front!" and he lifted up my towel. The handsome fella at the door laughed his ass off (who could blame him) and I quickly shut the door. After being mortified, I ran upstairs where the baby was now awake along with Ben who was begging for breakfast. I looked at the envelope, wondering what the hell could be so important and realized it was addressed to the next door neighbors' house. No joke. Fuck you air-mail delivery man, you prick! I threw on some sweats, put Jordan in his highchair and made breakfast. It wasn't until after lunch, four hours later when the baby went down for a nap, when I realized my hair was still full of conditioner. I jumped back in the shower to rinse it off so quickly that I think I literally held my breath the whole time, just in case I heard a cry, or a doorbell, or a damned singing telegram for that matter. It's a good thing I was quick because after holding my breath for too long, my kids would have found me drowned, face down, and naked in the shower. But even if they did, they would probably just laugh because they saw a naked butt.

From this story of chaos, I will find a bright side. My hair got a really, really good deep conditioning treatment. It was silky and soft and salon-beautiful...okay, maybe not salon-beautiful, but it was really soft. When it seems you can't accomplish even the most basic of tasks, when you think you are failing at life because you can't even get a proper shower, keep your chin up if your neck doesn't hurt too bad. Oh...and if your neighbor's mail ever comes to your house...just throw it in the fucking trash! It's not your fault it got delivered to the wrong address.

Thanks for reading!
~*V Bow*

Dr. Lipton sets the print out in his lap and takes off his glasses. "Now Vada, explain this to me. What were you feeling when you wrote this?"

Well genius, I think it's pretty self-explanatory, but I'll give it a shot. "It was a really funny situation that happened and I thought it was funny enough to blog about. I do have neck problems though, it's always stiff. I think it was a funny post...what seems to be your concern? Is it my neck?"

"Not at this particular moment, Vada. My concern is that you used the phrase 'failing at life.' Do you feel like life is pushing you down, Vada? You reference drowning. Do you feel like you are drowning Vada?"

Umm...really? Did this guy get his degree online for crying out loud? "Well, sometimes, I just...uhh...I just meant that it's hard to do simple things when you have children. I ended it on a positive note, didn't I?"

He looks at me sternly and almost disappointed. I want to flick him in the nose and call him an idiot.

I take a deep breath and my words spew out like Rita's supper, "Yes Dr. Lipton, I feel like I'm drowning. It feels like I am totally drowning and

I need rescued."

A huge smile crosses his lips, "Good Vada, this is excellent." Geez, I guess I said the right thing. He then continues his big blabber about coping and dealing and blah, blah, blah, and I am singing "God Bless America" in my head, because I need something that will drown out his voice. He finally finishes after questioning me one more time about whether I need cough or reflux medication. I tell him no. He then asks me how my neck feels today. I simply smile and say, "It's always a little sore, but I'm okay." He gives me a wave goodbye, puts his glasses back on, and turns back to his papers.

I shut the door behind me. I have to hurry and get out of here before I get a paper cut on my ass.

Janitorial Services

Once I get to my room I pull the chart out of the back of my pants. What a dumb idea that was. I wish I had never seen it in the first place. What if I get caught? I'm sure this violates all sorts of privacy rules. I guess since I am already at risk of getting in trouble, I might as well read it. I sit down in the big floral chair and grab it off the table. To my complete shock there is a small streak of blood across the top of the manila folder. I check myself for paper cuts, but nothing. How in the world did this get blood on it? Then it hit me. It's my heavy flow day. This is just fantastic. Absolutely perfect! That's what I get for sticking it in my pants. The only time in my life I have ever stuck a stolen medical chart in my pants, I menstruate on it. That's my life in a nutshell.

The thought grosses me out so much that I take out the contents and throw the folder into the wastebasket in the bathroom. A shower sounds good anyways, but even better now that I have to wash away the guilt I now carry from being a thief. After tossing a fresh super absorbency plug up the sub-basement, I throw on a fresh pair of under-britches, baggy sweats, and a sleeveless top. I carefully examine the papers, which fortunately have not been affected during the incident. I dig for dirt. It says here that this is Mary's second stay here at New Outlook. I know I should stop reading this, but I can't. Mary was diagnosed with bipolar as a child, trouble with peers, and trouble with authority. It says she is currently taking a cocktail of drugs to help with sexual compulsions and on lithium for bipolar. Hmm...I read on.

Weaverton has expressed being unhappy with her new roommate, Vada Bower. Request for roommate transfer will be granted pending administrative approval.

That bitch! She wanted *me* out? I gave her my pudding cup!

Her file is thick and filled with disgusting details of encounters with various men including several male teachers in high school and community college. She has been involved in countless sexual shenanigans with married men and was once married herself, to a truck driver, named Orville Merrifield. Who would have thought Bath Salts Mary could bag so many dudes? I've only been with one and I married him. This girl has put me to shame. Even though she's a home-wrecker, I've got to hand it to her. The girl gets her freak on. Funny that it doesn't say she's been with women although I know she was with one last night, but you know, we all have our secrets.

I feel I have done enough Magnum PI-ing for now and I fold up her papers and stick them in the bottom of my suitcase. Although, I'd still like to find out who this gal was who spent the night with her last night. I imagine it's just a sex thing and I should really just stay out of other people's business.

Katelyn comes in and says I have a visitor. She seems kind of giddy though, and I can't figure out why. She leads me to the room with the big double doors and I see my brother Heath sitting at a table. I expect him to hop up and hug me, but he doesn't. He is looking right past me. He is looking at Katelyn. Oh for crying out loud! He waves to her and I immediately glance back at her. She has this flirty little grin on her face and gives Heath a little finger wave, then heads out the door.

"Do I need to leave, so you can visit the nurse?" I ask.

"Shut up, Vada. What's her name anyways?" he asks.

"Katelyn. But I'm here, so if you'd like to ask me how I am doing in the hospital, I will answer you. If not, I can have her come back and sit with you and I'll get back to recovery."

"Oh yeah, well, I wanted to come check on my little sis and make sure you were okay. How are they treating you in here?"

I give him the rundown on the place and tell him I am fine. I also tell him that if anyone finds out I am here I will hurt him—badly. He fills me in on his latest moving jobs and says that business is pretty slow right now, but should pick up once it gets warmer. I'm really glad he came to visit me. It's nice to know that he cares and Heath doesn't judge. He's just a big brother checking up on his little sister and checking out his little sister's smokin' hot nurse.

After a good visit we hug goodbye. He tells me he's going to go see my boys and help out if they need him. I thank him very much and then out the double doors he goes, off to my home to see my kids. I want to go with him. I just want to kiss their faces.

I leave and walk to the Social Room. It has a lot to offer and I'm not being sarcastic. There are shelves lined with hundreds of books and board games to choose from. There is a ping pong table and an air hockey table over in the corner. The walls are decorated with artwork from patients over the years, some of which are quite good. There are paintings, sculptures made of clay, even some display cases with handmade jewelry. One drawing on the wall in a frame catches my eye. It was done in colored pencils and it's of a woman's face, but she has no mouth. Her eyes look so familiar and I feel like I know this girl. I study it for a while, and then make my way to an empty couch in the T.V. room. Lucky for me no one is watching it and there is a Kardashian marathon on!

After my fill of Khloe clearly being the funniest one, Scott being a dick to Kourteney, and Kim pouting, I decide to head back to my room. I stop and take one more look at this drawing and I get no further in my evaluation of who this is. There is no signature or date, but it sticks in my mind. I make my way down the long corridor towards 109 and I notice right away that my door is slightly ajar. I cautiously enter the room to find a tall man with a blonde ponytail standing there wearing latex gloves. He is not looking happy. Oh God! I hope this isn't like one of those prison shake downs and he's going to give me a cavity search. I'm allergic to latex. Wouldn't that be a fun rash!

"She told me about you!" he says. He looks vaguely familiar to me, but I can't place him. Maybe he's from the men's ward and he's escaped and he's going to strangle me. Maybe he thinks I am someone else. Maybe I am about to be murdered in a mental institution by a crazed lunatic. What are they going to tell my children? I'm so scared that I may possibly piss in my pants.

He repeats his words again, "She told me about you." His navy blue pants and white button down shirt don't necessarily make him look like he could be a patient here. It almost looks like he's...a janitor...yes, he works in housekeeping. Room 74 must be the janitor's room. This is the woman who was banging Bath Salts Mary last night! Eww. Only he is not a woman, he is a man. But, what the hell is he doing in my room?

"What the hell are you doing in my room?" I ask him, trying to sound tough and bad-ass. I'm using all sixty inches of height to intimidate him, although I'm not sure it is working.

"You tell me what you are doing with her chart first. And why the fuck is there blood on it. She said you were weird. Are you doing some sort of sacrificial obsession role-play thing or something? You stay away from her okay? You got that, you crazy bitch? I've seen people like you in here before."

Am I really hearing this? Am I really *hearing* this?

"You don't understand. It's all a mistake, just calm yourself down. First of all, I don't even know her, and second of all," I lie, "I didn't mean to take her chart. I thought it was my chart. I was trying to sneak it out from Dr. Lipton's office and I got the wrong one. I grabbed it so quick I got a really bad paper cut, okay? That's why there is blood on it."

He looked like he was buying it. He dropped his hands and his circus-like face softened a little.

"I think Ba-I mean Mary is a pretty nice lady from what I can tell. I have no problems with her. I wish she was fonder of me. I know she doesn't like me, but I'll stay out of her way. I didn't even know she had a boyfriend."

"What?" he says angrily, "Who's this boyfriend? If she's lying to me then I'll..."

"No, no I meant you. What is your name?"

"Jeremiah."

"I meant you, Jeremiah. I didn't know you and she were in a relationship."

"Well, we are and things was going just fine till you showed up and then I couldn't have my overnights with 'er. Once you came and we couldn't sleep together she didn't even wanna see me. Nows that the doctors have seen how crazy you are...they locked you up in here, I finally got her back. Good thing they put you alone. Serves you right."

"Okay, that was quite rude...and wait just a minute, Mr. Clean. Does the hospital know that you're banging one of the patients? Is that in your job description next to cleaning floors? Hmm...I wonder if the administration would care to hear that after you empty the trash, you stick your dick in it."

Ooh...I wonder if he has a carpet cleaner...the floor in my room could use a good scrubbing and I won't walk on it with bare feet. I realize I am standing on my tip-toes and my feet hurt in these flip flops. I go and sit down and ask him to have a seat so we can work out a little deal. These floral patterned chairs are really coming in a lot handier than I would have predicted. He's the one who looks scared now and I know I am in control of this situation. I'm starting to feel a little bad for the guy; he looks like he may cry.

"Jeremiah, I'm not going to tell anyone. Calm down."

He looks relieved as hell and gives a really goofy smile revealing some extremely neglected teeth. "So you think that we can keep this thing between us? Hell, I just came in here to empty your trashcans and run the sweeper."

"Well, I'd like to ask you just a few more questions, Jeremiah."

"Make it quick, crazy lady, 'cause I got the whole rest of hall to do and I'd like to clean myself up before I see Mary tonight."

"Alright, knock the 'crazy lady' shit off. Your girlfriend's the one... oh never mind. What's the point? Listen, I think I can help you with Mary."

His eyes light up. He looks like a baby getting ready to take in a spoon full of mashed apricot dessert from a jar, the poor bastard.

"You need to make her feel special. You need to spend the night with her tonight with *no* sex."

"How's come you think you know what I should do?" he asks.

Oh my gosh, he's so stupid. "I'm just giving you some advice, if you don't want it then don't take it."

"But wait just one dang minute. Did you say no sex? What the hell? Then what the hell are we supposed to do? Just rub each other's privates with our hands?"

The mental picture I just got means I'm skipping dinner and will probably skip foreplay for the rest of my life. Oh well, at least Eric's going to benefit from this.

"No. Look at me...I said *no*. No boob action and nothing down south either (which in her case is all pretty much the same). Nothing but smooching." I am doing my best to speak his language. Ol' Jeremiah ain't none too bright. "Here's exactly what you are going to do, now quit sitting here looking at me like you have a leech on your nuts, this is not the first time in history a guy has ever stayed with a girl without having sex."

"Well, then what the hell we s'posed to do? Play checkers?"

"Umm...why not? There's a checkers game in the Social Room. Do you get a break before your shift ends?"

"Not a scheduled one, but I can take fifteen here and there."

"Listen up then. When we are done talking, which I hope to be soon, I want you to run to that little gas station, I think it called the "Fill-Trip" down on the corner before the interstate. I want you to go buy those little roses that come individually wrapped, get twelve of them, but for Pete's sake take the wrappers off. Get a bottle of wine, but hide it good. Use the paper cups we get for rinsing our teeth as your wine glasses. Tonight you and Mary are going to have a date; wine and roses and games. Then lie down next to her and tell her how you really feel about her. See, Jeremiah, she needs to know that you want more than sex from her. You do, don't you?"

"Yes ma'am I sure do. I never liked anyone so bad in all my life."

"She needs to know that. You and I both know I've seen her chart. I think she needs a meaningful relationship. She needs to feel like you care about her, so try this and just see how it goes."

"Whatever you say ma'am. I'll try anything."

"I'm afraid I'm going to need access to the janitor's closet as well. You do a piss poor job of keeping these floors clean and in order to keep my mouth shut about this, I'm going to need some cleaning supplies. Got it?"

He looks confused, but pulls a key off of his bungee cord key chain. It must be a spare. He gets up from the chair and heads for the door, slowly, like he's trying to remember everything on his to-do list.

"Oh and Jeremiah...one more thing to get at the store..."

"What is it?"

"Something chocolate...and with caramel...and King Size."

"Okay, I can do that. You sure she likes chocolate?"

"Oh no Jeremiah, that's for me. You can leave it on my dresser."

Assorted Nuts

Oh, what a day this has been! Things were not supposed to get this complicated. I have a group session and maybe dinner if I get my appetite back. I'm just ready for my meds and then I can go to sleep. Tomorrow I will go to yoga and then see about leaving this place hopefully within the next day or so. I'm starting to *really* miss my boys, all four of them.

For now, I am going to rest for forty-five minutes. After I am all power-napped and yawned out, I decide to call Sabrina. She says she's been worried about me being in trouble for our little "party" the other day. I tell her everything is fine and she tells me to let her know if I need anything, anything at all. She tells me that my boys are crazy and that Ben was in trouble when she went over there to check on them. Apparently, he decided that it would be a really exciting to try and clean the bathroom with hand soap. Sink, toilet, floors, walls and all. I guess the bathroom was so covered in Warm Vanilla Sugar bubbles that Eric shut the door and waited until my mother got there because he didn't know what to do. I guess I am needed after all. Hell, that wouldn't even bother me because it is soap. If it was syrup, or hair, or some other fluidy substance, it might put me in the fetal position and I'd be trying to pull out one of my canine teeth. However, soap is not a problem for me. I say, "Way to go Ben!" You clean that bathroom. If I were home, he wouldn't have been in trouble. I would have simply showed him my Swiffer and Clorox wipes and we'd have had a good time. So I guess if that's the worst thing that's happened, they are in pretty good shape.

I check my face and curl my eyelashes to look alive. I throw on a gray sweatshirt and yoga pants to blend in, and then head to the Solarium. This group session tonight is not just for the pukers. It's a delicious concoction of the depressed and manics, the obsessives, the compulsives, and the addicts. It's for the anti-socials, the narcissists, the hair-pullers, the hair-eaters, (hopefully not sitting next to each other) and the phobics. It's like a circus full of freaks and the group session is, in theory, to let us know that we are all in this together. It's my first one of this kind and I am actually quite excited to see what goes on, although I plan to keep my mouth shut and just listen. This is not a required event, but why not go? When in Rome...

This is a decent turn out I would assume, although I have nothing to base it on. At least it looks like it. I'm guessing maybe forty of us sitting in the beautiful Solarium. All I can think now is that I should have brought a hand mirror. I would gaze in it and say, "Mirror mirror on the wall, who's the craziest of us all?" Actually scratch that. I'm too afraid I would see my own reflection. And scientifically speaking, I would.

There are small trays of food placed around on the tables. I see mini-sandwiches and fruits and veggies with dip. I also see some bowls of assorted nuts, which is just fucking mean, given the situation we are in. Maybe I take things too personally. I find a cozy spot next to a beautiful and overweight woman who seriously has the prettiest face I have ever seen. Her black hair is wavy and shoulder-length. It is so shiny you can almost see your reflection bounce off of it. She has olive skin, bright green eyes with thick, long eyelashes, pretty full red lips, and I am completely awestruck by her beauty. She gives me a sweet smile and sits quietly. She must be a newbie too because she seems a bit out of place. I look around for anyone I might recognize. I see Jessalyn walk in, but she doesn't see me and sits on a purple chaise lounge over in the corner. I do recognize a couple ladies I have seen at dinner, including the ones who ate my brownies. I wonder if it would be awkward if I talked to them now. Why would I, though? I'm not here to make friends.

The quiet noise of small talk comes to a halt when a tall and pretty black woman stands up. She is probably in her late forties and dressed in a purple suit.

"Good evening, ladies. I'd like to thank you all for coming to this session tonight. My name is Amelia Peters. As you may know, I am the administrator here at New Outlook. This particular group therapy activity is a relatively new idea. We believe that by exploring new methods of therapy and communication, we are giving our patients a better chance of recovery. By hearing the stories of others, even if they are different than yours, you will gain an understanding of what your peers are going through. My hope is that it may help you gain a better understanding of your own illnesses and experiences."

The pretty lady and I are both on our second sandwich at this point. They are just little ones, for crying out loud. I have figured out these are turkey and Swiss, and it looks like the table down from us has some sort of BLT situation going on. I'm going to need to investigate this further as no one informed me there was bacon in the building. I get up half way and my back is in an arch. I look like I am trying to dodge gunfire, but at least I'm making my way to the next table. Trying hard not to make eye contact, I grab up two BLT's and shimmy my way back to my seat. I hand one to my new girlfriend sitting next to me who smiles gratefully and we enjoy. These were worth the trip.

I actually realize there are people standing up and talking. I must have zoned them out. I try my damndest to pay attention. An elderly woman goes on about her days as a prostitute and how she used to lot lizard the truck stops in Toledo. She has maybe two teeth that I can see, and she probably made a good living like that. Lots of fellas like the toothless gals at the truck stops from what I've heard on day-time talk shows. Apparently Ol' Granny Gum-Some-Cum is having a hard time dealing with her loss of self-respect, so she's taken to the meth. Well, that is not going to help her dental situation, but I guess you've got to give her some credit for standing up here talking about it. Apparently, this is her last stop on the intervention train. Her family has agreed to pay for her stay here as long as she'll turn her life around. I just hope that if she makes it through recovery, they'll throw in a set of dentures.

Next up I have the pleasure of hearing about a post-partum mom who is also anxiety-ridden and has "germ" issues. Well, welcome to the club lady. I hear a few more. One burns herself with a lighter because she is lonely, and the poor girl has scars all over her body. Another rises and tells her story about being bullied her whole life and now she is afraid to leave her house. The real dandy is the girl who thinks she can speak in tongues. I shit you not she starts off saying she's been in here for two months and her new medications are hard to get used to. Then BAM! All of a sudden she breaks out into what sounds like she's speaking Arabic but in Pig-Latin. Awkward. I pass on my turn. I'm too busy eating.

Oh, this is fun. What a real treat. I get to come here and listen to all of this and eat sandwiches. Now this is what I'm talking about. Then, in walks the woman I saw today in the yard. This is the birthday girl who had the psychosis. She has her arm in a loop with Gerri the plastic faced nurse and she sits in a chair and just listens. Now I feel like crap. Surely, she won't talk. Why are they bringing her in here after what happened earlier? Much to my surprise, she raises her hand. She stands.

"My name is Lauren Sanders. Today is my birthday." She looks a mess. Her eyes look empty and it's almost like she's a mannequin, but one that is talking.

Why is she doing this?

"I was born in a shack in Kentucky and I barely survived my birth. My mother delivered me herself without a doctor. Doctors are shitheads. She reached right inside her gigantic vagina after fifteen hours of labor and pulled me out with her bare hands. My mother had to chew the chord off with her teeth. She wrapped me in newspaper because we had no blankets. They were hanging on the line to dry. There was no food in the house and so she had to eat the placenta for nourishment and then fed me from her large and lactating bosoms."

Some of the women are laughing and Nurse Gerri immediately raises her hand to shush them. I realize my mouth is hanging open. I have to force myself to shut it. Oh my goodness, she's not done with the story.

"I know I am a miracle. I am the product of a natural childbirth. We lived in the woods, you know. We lived off the land." She looks down at the floor and sways back and forth. "I ate a squirrel once. I ate beaver too."

I can't take it. I try to hold back, but I blow a huge gust of laughter from my mouth that sounds like a chicken sneeze. I try my best to play it off like it allergies. I itch my nose and say, "Excuse me, must be the ragweed in the air."

Lauren keeps going, "My doctors here are shitheads. Today is my birthday. Did anyone hear me?" She's getting louder. "I said today is MY BIRTHDAY! I was born in Kentucky! I'm a miracle!"

Oh shit, she's yelling. Gerri takes her by the hand and leads her out of the room. I can hear her singing Happy Birthday to herself as she is calmly escorted out the door. Wow. That was awesome. And yet, I feel really sorry for her, she is so sad. I wonder if that story is true, but mostly I wonder why she uses the word, bosom.

A Plan for Katelyn

After group, I decide to eat dinner in my room. They bring me a tray of lasagna and garlic bread and a banana. I hate red sauce and I am allergic to bananas. They make my lips swell up like a vagina with an infection. I'm not hungry anyway since I ate all those sandwiches. But I do need dessert and I see that Jeremiah, aka, Romeo the Janitor has fulfilled my request with a King Size Caramello. It is truly the only thing that helps me during that time of the month. I sit in my quiet room and have an intimate encounter with my candy bar. Almost naughty...if you consider naughty to be biting softly on the tip and then sucking it until it explodes in my mouth. That totally hits the spot...every time.

I hear a knock on my door and in walks Katelyn. She has my little white cup. There is a new pill in there, but I don't even bother asking what it's for. Dr. Lipton probably thinks I need it and that's good enough for me.

"Katelyn, where have you been all day?" I ask like it's any of my business.

"I've been having ex-issues and I just don't know what to do anymore. He wants me back."

"Hahaha! Well I hope you told him where to stick it...and I hope it wasn't in *you*! You aren't taking him back, are you? Tell me you are not taking him back."

"No...I umm...I am not taking him back. I just don't know what to do. I'm so screwed, so broke...and so depressed. What am I going to do, Vada?"

Here it comes again. I am now the caregiver and this poor girl needs to be cared for. Once again, I invite yet another of my "patients" to sit in my floral patterned chairs.

"Listen to my face, Katelyn! I think I have an answer for you. So the guy took your money? He has ruined your credit and your life?"

She looks at me, nodding, and there is a smudge on the right eye and a tiny one on the left. Her hair is still perfect, in a braided bun at the top of her head. Not one fly-away.

"He took me for everything. Everything I worked so hard for is gone. He's living in my damn apartment! I put myself through nursing school for pity sake. I thought I was actually making something of myself. I promised myself I would never be in the abusive relationships that my mother was in all of those years I was growing up."

I feel my inner counselor coming out. I ask, "What happened to your mom, Katelyn?"

"Well, I don't know who my father is, for one thing. The first guy she dated was a total jerk. He was always drunk with his shirt off. He'd come home from work and start drinking and after about six or seven beers he'd start his rages. He used to throw her around and bruise her up pretty bad. She finally got rid of him, only because he left her. I think he had his fill and went on to the next woman he could bully. The next guy was a real winner too."

"Well, what happened to him?"

"He's my step-dad I guess. They are still married. He still hurts her, but she allows it. I've tried to get her to leave like a hundred times, but she thinks he needs her. How messed up is that? But you know what? I never wanted to be like that and now I'm in the same situation. Except Michael, my ex, has only hit me a couple of times"

"Katelyn, he hits you too? What are you thinking?"

"I know. I know, okay? Why do you think my make-up is so thick? I don't need a lecture from you. No offense, Vada, but you are the one in a mental institution."

"Good point. But Katelyn...I know how to get back at him. Just write down your apartment address and leave the rest to me."

"Oh no. Vada, this is not okay. I am your nurse. Don't get involved in my messes."

"Would you shut up and just trust me? I know what I'm doing, for crying out loud, Katelyn. Let someone help you. You take care of people every day."

"Technically, Vada, so do you. You have three little boys."

"I know this, so trust me. Now write it down and go take care of the rest of your patients."

She reluctantly jots down her address and tells me goodnight. Out the big creaky door she goes.

I immediately get on the phone with my brother Heath. I tell Heath I need a huge favor and it involves that hot nurse, Katelyn from my looney bin. He is more than happy to oblige.

March 6th

I wake up and have meds and breakfast, which is cereal and that makes me miss my kids. My kids do eat cereal. I totally lied to Dr. Lipton about that. He bought it. I call Eric and check on things. He is missing me and I can hear in his voice that the pressure of me not being there is tough on him. He's only had to miss a day of work here and there since my mother is staying with them, so I'll give him the benefit of the doubt that it is hard. Really, though, at least he has help.

"You feeling better baby? Any word on when you will be released?"

"Soon, kid. I have a couple things I still need to take care of here and then I will be home."

"You take as long as you need. We just want you better. But what is it exactly that you have to take care of?"

"Oh..." I catch myself, "Just a few more therapists want to check me for ligature marks and things."

"Haha, very funny. You wanna talk to the boys?"

"Of course, I do!" I say.

A sweet little voice comes on the line; it's Ben, "Hi, Mommy. Did you know that Lebron James is the best dunker in the NBA?"

"Oh really!" I say. "Did you know that you are the sweetest six year-old that I've ever known?"

"Mom, that was so nice. You are a princess. When are you coming home because Daddy doesn't make my waffles right. They are too crunchy and...I...I...try to tell him but he just doesn't listen, see, he's not a good listener."

"I know baby. He is not a good listener. I'll talk to him about that okay? How's everything at school? Are you doing okay?"

"Yeah, Mommy, I'm great except I just have trouble listening sometimes and I have to walk laps at recess. I think I'm like that because I get it from my dad. He's not a good listener too. I think God should have made our ears bigger."

"Your ears are just fine. Try your best okay? Just do what your teacher says. I'll be so proud of you! Try to be the best listener in the whole wide world, like even better than the man with the biggest ears on the Earth!"

"Okay Mommy, Max wants to talk to you. Love you. Bye."

Before I can even say anything, he hands the phone off and Max says, "Mommy! Please come home because Ben told me is going to tape my butt cheeks together!"

"Max, he will not do that."

"Yes he will, and then I won't be able to go poop and I'll have poop stuck in my butt for the rest of my life! What if it gets so full it comes out my nose?"

"Max, listen to me...I will tell Daddy to make sure that doesn't happen. Okay? Forget about it. How are you, baby?"

"Just great, Mommy. I'm just freaking great."

Oh my, Max is just like me! "Max, don't say freaking. Is school okay?"

"Yeah, but I'm getting sick of going every day. I think it's freaking weird that it takes up the whole day!"

"Max, I said don't say freaking. Well, honey, I love your face. I miss you and go kiss yourself for me, okay?"

"How am I supposed to do that? You are so crazy, Mommy."

He's right. "I love you buddy, now let me talk to Jordan."

He hands the phone to Jordan and I catch a few "mamas" in there. He makes my heart melt. Then Eric takes back the phone.

"Alright, VadieGirl. The kids all ran off and I need to go find them, but I love you and call me tonight before bed, okay?"

"Okay, love you too, kid. Hey, don't let Ben tape Max's butt cheeks together, okay? And quit making Ben's waffles so crunchy."

"Oh, I heard all about it. I won't. You should have seen them earlier. They played rock paper scissors to see who the biggest loser was. I played with them and I won."

"Well, that seems pretty accurate, but you know that's encouraging them to use words like "loser". You shouldn't fucking do that!"

"I know. Sorry baby. Love you."

"Love you too. Bye."

Bring on the tears. I miss the smell of my laundry. I miss the smell of Eric when he gets out of the shower. I miss the smell of my babies' sweet faces when they snuggle with me in the morning. But I know it won't be long before I am home. This whole thing is turning out very different than I had planned, but it is what it is. I just have to go with it.

Looking over my quack schedule I have nothing until noon, which is a session with Dr. Ames. Yippee. I shower and slip on my yoga pants and a tank top in case I can get in on a yoga class with all my free time this morning. I leave my hair down today and wavy. Why not change it up a bit? Feeling good and relaxed from whatever benzo I got, I open my door and lo and behold, guess what I find? A note. Oh great, who's on to me now?

-Vada Bower-

Jeremiah told me everything. But I forgive you. I wanted you to know that his loving arms held onto me like an Eskimo baby in a snow storm, so safe and so warm all through the night. And I want to thank you for not harming me. He told me about the blood and that he convinced you to let him have me. I knew you were in love with me the moment you looked at me. That day when I came out of the hot tub and I saw the way you lusted after my body, was painful to watch. I felt so sorry for you. I know it must have been hard to let me go to a man, especially as mentally ill as you are. Jeremiah told me that you wish I was fonder of you, but you are simply not my type. I'm not attracted to you. But I'd like to thank you for being unselfish. I'd still like to ask that you keep your distance. I wouldn't want him to see you looking at me and get the wrong idea. Maybe once this blows over, we could be friends. Maybe not. We will see. But be warned, I'll be keeping an eye on you.

Good day, Mary Weaverton

Well, isn't that just great...just freaking great? So she thinks I'm in love with her. I will never give my pudding cup away again. Clearly, it sends the wrong message. At least I may get to be a bridesmaid. I must admit, I'm a little bruised on my ego that she's not attracted to me. If I can't even land Bath Salts Mary, I must be a real dog. Sheesh, I feel like I must be in a goddam looney bin.

Ducks and Quacks

I head off in search of a morning adventure. Actually, I head off in search of some peace and quiet. I could do the yoga but from the looks of the participants, I really don't to be close to them if they are bending over. I'm just going to take a walk. The clouds are rolling in and I can smell the raindrops forming in the sky. It's only a few sprinkles, and for some reason, it makes me want to keep walking. I head down a path and watch a mother duck and her five little ducklings hop into the lake. The mother looks incredibly nervous and her head is moving back and forth, and I believe she is doing a headcount. They stay close to their mother and this little gal reminds me very much of myself. She is freaking out, worrying about them. Out here, she has to protect her babies from the weather. She has to make sure they have enough to eat, and of course protect them from other animals. I begin to think that mother ducks are actually lucky. They don't have the pressures we human mothers do. Yes, we have to keep them alive, but we also have to keep our babies safe from every possible evil in this world; child molesters, germs, bullies, senseless acts of violence, social media, media in general, wars, and every other terrifying thing that humans have to be afraid of. I wonder if the mother duck needs a Xanax. I imagine she made her home in this mental ward for a reason. I personally prefer these quacks over the ones inside.

The rain begins to fall harder. I say farewell to my new duck friends. Instead of walking back to the building, I walk further down the trail. The rain continues to fall. Big drops, not little ones and I am getting soaking wet. In true classic Vadie luck, the one day I leave my hair down and it actually looks cute, it gets soaking wet. I really don't care. It feels so good not to care. There is no one I feel I need to impress. There is no one looking at me, judging how I am disciplining or not disciplining my children. I feel no guilt for not folding laundry or not unloading the dishwasher. I feel no pressure to be attending every function we are invited to and having to have something cute to wear to it. All I feel is this awesome spring rain. I look up to the sky and throw my hands up in the air. The rain feels like it is washing my guilt away, washing my pressure away, washing away the feelings that overwhelm me. I feel like this is the reason I am here, this is where I need to be right now in this moment...I think I am finding peace...

"Miss...excuse me...miss, umm...there is lightning in the area and we are under a severe thunderstorm warning, so I'm going to have to ask you to please come indoors immediately." A scrawny male security guard with a black umbrella is hollering at me. "The outdoor area is being closed down until the warnings are lifted." I tell him to fuck off and then I beat him with the umbrella. Not really, I didn't say or do that. But sonofabitch! Are you kidding me? I put my rejoicing arms back down by my side and walk all hunched over and pissed off back to the building, where I am now left with a rat's nest of wet hair and coincidentally, no hair tie on my wrist.

After my one and only "zen" moment being interrupted by the storm and the weather cop, I go back to my room and change into dry clothes. I choose a snuggly KU sweatshirt and running shorts. I grab a hair tie and throw my hair up in a ball. I pick a book from the Social Room, a book about witches and wizards. I'm ordinarily not into those kinds of books, but today I just want to try something different. I take it to the Solarium and curl up with a cup of coffee. The storm is really beating down and I think about my boys. I know they are not afraid of storms, but I just hope they are safe. Sometimes I take them to the basement anyways "to play" just in case. Hey, when you live in the Midwest, tornadoes happen. I hope that Eric has them playing downstairs.

Reading with the sounds of rain is a relaxing experience and I'm sure that I may actually be enjoying myself. I look up and Lauren Sanders is walking past me. She sits on a bench in the bay window and looks out. Crap, it's raining on her "birthday..."

I abandon my coffee and book and I slowly walk over to the bench, which is long enough for three people, so I just act like I came to watch the rain. I can see she is crying.

"Hey...um," I say nervously, "My name is Vada."

"Hello, I am Lauren." She is wiping her eyes and trying to smile.

"I heard you talk last night in group and I just wanted to tell you, Happy Birthday."

"Thanks, shithead," she says and then looks back out the window.

Should I get up? Should I go back and read? Then she turns and looks at me and smiles. She actually looks pretty normal when she smiles. Her hair is chestnut brown and shoulder length. Up close, I can see she has freckles and is actually kind of cute. She has prominent laugh lines around her smile. She almost reminds me of a junior high schooler in an awkward phase, only she's an adult and schizophrenic...really though, what's the difference?

"Did you just say what I think you said?" she asks.

She looks at me bewildered and I don't know if she's going to start swinging at me or hug me. She stands up and says, "Come, follow me."

She takes me down the long hallway, a separate wing from mine with much nicer carpet. It looks brand new and spotless. I'm walking behind her and I realize I am shaking because my nervous anxiety is about to completely overtake me. She stops at 214 and opens her door. Her room is pretty similar to my own. It's a single with a sitting area and a bathroom. I take a seat and she goes over and pulls out a box from under the bed. It's a photo box, red and green plaid.

She motions me over and before I know it we are both sitting criss-cross applesauce on her bed and she is showing me pictures. There are pictures from her birthday parties growing up. It looks like she had a fairly good set of birthday parties in her life and maybe she just can't let them go.

"Is that your husband?"

"That was my husband, until the bastard left me for some woman that he got pregnant, while we were married. She has large bouncing bosoms," she says angrily.

There is that word again! "Well, my goodness, Lauren, I am so sorry to hear that."

We keep looking through pictures. I notice that her mother is in the photos when she is just a little girl, and she did appear to have a large rack, but then it appears she is with different families. Interesting. Where is her mother in the rest of these photos?

"Lauren, forgive me if I sound nosy, but who are these people with you in these pictures?"

She pulls one out. "That was my first foster family. They were shitheads." This photo is a young Lauren with a man, woman and twin boys. They look pretty normal. "Here is the second." She hands me another picture of herself only a little older and standing with an elderly looking couple. "And this was my last one and I killed them," she says.

Oh bloody hell! I am with a murderer on her birthday. Oh my Lord, be with me. I need to get out of this room.

"I didn't kill them...on purpose. You see, they took me in after the second family got sick of me and then Papa Rick, that's what I called him and Mama JoAnn, that's what I called her, well they got in a car wreck and died. They were the only ones who ever really loved me, besides my mother. They never could have children of their own, so they got me instead. I know they wanted a child like me. They wanted one who was natural and able to hunt. We used to go hunting together."

"Oh I am so sorry, Lauren! That must have been terrible for you, how old were you?"

"I was just about to turn sixteen when they died. I have lived in group homes ever since. I keep telling these shitheads that I can take care of myself. I know how to hunt and I can make a place for myself down at the river."

Shit, this is just awful. "So Lauren, what happened to your birth mother?"

"She was too poor to take care of me and turned me over to the state. But I know she loved me. She kept me alive as long as she could. She dropped me off at a center when I was eight years old." Lauren looks so sad, and then she smiles and says "It's my birthday today!"

"I know, Lauren! Happy birthday!" Then suddenly, I have a thought. "Lauren, would it be okay if I came back around five this afternoon to visit?"

She looks confused. "Yeah, sure," she says, "See ya then."

I stand up and give her a hug and head for the door.

"Hey, shithead," she says and I turn around briefly, "thanks for looking at my pictures."

"Anytime."

She smiles and I shut the door softly behind me. I think we have just become bosom buddies.

Hypnosis

I head to Dr. Ames' office for my noon session.

"Hello, Miss Vada," he says as I come and sit on the comfy couch.

"Hello," I say back.

"You look a little uneasy today, a little nervous perhaps. Is everything okay?"

No, everything's not okay. I just had a sit down with the orphaned birthday girl who eats beavers and loves bosoms, and I don't know what to

101

think. I don't even know what the hell just happened back there.

"Yes, everything is fine. Rainy day, huh?"

"Yes, everyone around here seems to have a hard time on these rainy days," he says with a smile.

Well, apparently everyone but you, doc. You seem pretty happy, but I'm guessing it is because you just ate what smells like a Reuben sandwich for lunch, and there's a little piece of sauerkraut hanging from your big fat mouth.

"Oh, not me. I love the rain!" I say.

"Good then. We are going to try some hypnotherapy today, Miss Vada. That means that I will be putting you under hypnosis. It's nothing to be alarmed about, just relax and keep an open mind. Before we begin, I have one more question. No more suicidal thoughts, correct?"

Only if I have to see that kraut hanging from your chin for much longer. It may actually drive me crazy enough where I have to hang myself with your lamp cord because it's so gross and you are making me not want to live.

"Of course not, Dr. Ames, I'm not anywhere near that frame of mind. Actually, since coming here, I think I may be better off than I realized."

"Well then, that's wonderful. Are you ready to begin with the hypnosis Vada?"

My Sam Kinison internal dialogue kicks in...YES, but get the fucking briny pickled cabbage off your motherfucking faaaaaace!!!

"Yes, let's rock and roll Dr. Ames."

"Hmm...I like your enthusiasm. Vada, do you remember how we

talked about this being your safe place? Your box? (haha) I want you to feel completely relaxed. Do you feel completely relaxed Vada?"

I nod.

"I'm going to ask you to picture a place where you feel the most comfortable in the world. The only noise you can hear is my voice."

I'm imagining being curled up in my bed with Eric and my boys all sleeping and I can hear Dr. Ames' voice. This must be working.

"Okay Vada, when I count down from ten you will fall asleep. Remember you are safe, relaxed, and remember to listen to my voice....10, 9, 8, 7, 6, 5, 4, 3, 2.......

"Vada, are you with me? Are you back in my room? In Dr. Ames' office?"

"Yes. Am I done? Did you already do it?

"Yes Vada. We are all finished. How are you feeling?"

"I'm feeling rested I guess. Well thanks a lot Dr. Ames. That was fun, a real good time. I hope I didn't say anything stupid."

"Oh Vada, I do not judge. You did reveal some things to me. Do you recall what you experienced?"

"Honestly, no I don't. Will you tell me?"

"Vada, or Vadie as you refer to yourself, I will, but I think it is best that I talk to Dr. Lipton and some of the other therapists before I have you recall that information. I don't want to alarm you. It is nothing serious, just standard procedure following hypnotherapy."

"Well...okay Dr. Ames. I guess I will see you next time."

"Next time, Miss Vada," and he nods with a goofy-ass smile as I walk out the door.

I do know one thing. I must have told him there was sauerkraut stuck to his face because it was gone when I came out of hypnosis.

I walk out of the room and notice Gerri, the plastic-face nurse, immediately entering his office and she shuts the door behind her. Something strikes me as odd about this. Call it an intuition, but I walk backwards until I am next to his office. The blinds are pulled so I can't see in, but I press my ear up to the door. I hope nobody catches me trying to listen in. Just when I think I am wasting my time and need to mind my own business, I hear a moaning sound. It's Gerri. I swear there is more action in this nuthouse than in a cathouse! He's married. He's a scumbag.

"Fuck me like a whore!"

That was Gerri's voice. Did she really just say that? Eww...so gross. I don't like the thought of the two of them getting it on, but I can only imagine it would be similar to him humping a blow-up doll. This is too much for me. I just came out of hypnosis; I need to wrap my mind around this. It's really none of my business, but I hate cheaters. I'm not going to say anything because I don't want to start trouble, but he's a pig and have no respect for him...or her for that matter.

I can't imagine saying that to Eric. I must be so lame. I can't imagine what breakfast would be like the next morning after asking him to screw me like a whore the night before. I can just see the kids around the table and myself filling up juice glasses and pouring cereal. I'd probably have to eat breakfast in the other room, because I couldn't look him in the eye. Poor Eric, I am so dull.

I'm getting ready to move along and pull my ear away from the door, when I feel an itching in my nose, I can't hold it back. I sneeze, a big loud sneeze. Shit! I stand frozen. I don't want them to see my footsteps outside the door. I hear nothing but silence. Their noisy screwing seems to have come to a halt due to my involuntary expulsion of nose air. They heard me. In a state of panic I take off down the hallway. I don't know where to go. I just hope they didn't know it was *me,* who was listening in.

I am disturbed, but I shake it off and decide to look for Jessalyn. The rain has stopped. I check the Social Room and find her sitting alone and drawing with colored pencils.

"Hey, you lady," I say.

"Look who it is...the mysterious Vada."

"So when in the hell are you busting out of this place?" I ask.

"Tomorrow actually." She looks down.

"Why don't you look excited?"

"I called my aunt for a ride and to see if I can stay with her and all she can talk about is this damn birthday party for my grandfather. Blah...so what was this big "idea" of yours anyways?"

"You really wanna hear it?"

"Hell, what have I got to lose besides the six pounds I've worked so hard to gain?"

"Ha ha...very funny, you skinny little bitch. I think I have an idea for a present on your grandfather's birthday."

"Not cool, Vada. What are you talking about?"

"Look, I know that drawing over there in the frame is yours, I can tell

105

because she looks like you and clearly, you draw." I pointed to what she was drawing now, which looks kind of like a superhero lady with huge muscles and a cape.

"Yeah, so what?"

"Well, she's missing a mouth, stupid. I think you should get a present on his birthday, not him. It's time to give you a voice. We are going to expose that sick prick for what he really is. No wonder you are such a damn mess, no offense, but you've kept this secret all these years for him! For him! Not for yourself. You said the other night you wanted to talk about it and I think it's time, don't you?"

"What's the point now Vada? He's so old and it's over."

"But it's not over for you, Jess. If it was over for you, you wouldn't be in this place getting help. You are still suffering after all these years. I say we let him suffer for a while, hell he's ninety anyways, he ain't gonna live forever."

"I may have to think about this..."

"Of course. Think about it and let me know. I'm here to help if you decide to go through with it."

Jessalyn sits quietly and stares out the window, twirling her hair. I grab her hand and give it a comforting squeeze, and then get up to leave. She grabs it tighter, pulls me back and says, "Vada, I've thought about it long enough. Let's show everyone who their hero really is."

I immediately make a call to Sabrina. Like I said, she's there whenever I need her. I give her instructions and tell her I will make every effort to meet her tomorrow night. We have a party to crash, and I've got to think of a way to sneak out of here.

Mission for Cake

I am now on a mission to find some cake. I walk back toward the kitchen area and find two ladies straight from lunch lady land preparing the trays for tonight's dinner. The larger one with glasses is going on about how her children never call unless they need something. She says that's all she's been good for over the years, free babysitting or money out her savings to help with car repairs. The little one is scooping out some sort of cherry pie filling into cups. Hmm...wonder what that's for. It looks good. I don't think little lunch lady is listening to a single word big lunch lady is saying. She's just concentrating on her task.

I walk up slowly and pull out a gun. I'm just kidding. I walk up slowly and clear my throat to get their attention. They both look up surprised.

"Hi ladies, how are you today?" I ask as sweet as sugar.

They look at each other almost frightened. I wonder if any of the crazies have ever talked to them before. I'm guessing that would be a no, considering their deer in headlights looks.

"Should we call security?" says big lunch lady to little lunch lady.

"Umm...really, I'll leave. I just needed a favor and I thought I would just see if you could help me out with something. If it's too much trouble then never mind."

Big lunch lady turns to little lunch lady and says, "See, even the crazy girl only comes to talk to us if she needs something."

"Oh, now you be nice, Gloria," says little lunch lady. "What can we help you with, sweetie?"

Ooh yay. Now I'm sweetie. Little lunch lady likes me and now we are getting somewhere.

"Well, I have a friend, see, and I really need a cake."

"Oh dear Lord, she must be one of them crazy schizophrenic women and she has an imaginary friend. I'm calling security." Gloria throws her hands up and heads for the phone, her jowls shaking this way and that in frustration.

"Stop it Gloria, right now. I'm sick of you always thinking everyone's out to get you all the time, always complaining. This girl looks no more crazy then you or me. Well, at least me." Ouch.

Gloria, although obviously annoyed at the situation, decides to pipe down.

"Alright, sweetie, my name is Loretta and you just tell me what kind of cake you need," says little lunch lady.

Loretta sounds like she may be from the south. She's a little bitty old grandma with gray hair that's probably long, but is tucked in a twist behind her head. She has on hot pink lipstick and pink cheeks to match. Her eyebrows are drawn on in brown pencil, which doesn't match her hair, but does seem to match her sweet personality. I think she's as cute as a bug and lucky for me she's kind of feisty too.

"Thank you so much ma'am. I need a white sheet cake with pink icing."

"Come back in an hour, sugar, and I'll have it ready," Loretta says with a hot pink smile.

Gloria just goes back to her trays shaking her head, mumbling under her breath like one of them crazy schizophrenic women.

My Gang

So now that I have a cake ordered, I'm not sure what to do next. I figure that if I'm going to throw Lauren Sanders a birthday party, I can't do it alone. I need to recruit New Outlook's finest. I must gather the elite society of the mentally ill. Of course I snatch up Jessalyn, who is busy preparing letters for tomorrow, but she can take an hour. I fill her in on the plan and then she and I go on a search. Where do the cool kids hang out in the asylum? Jessalyn tells me she has seen Lauren hanging out with a panic attack chick and they seem to have become chummy. I don't know her name but I'm calling her Panicky Pearl. We find her and invite her along. She seems pleasant enough and whatever kind of dope they have her on must be working because she doesn't seem to be panicking, at least for the moment. I ask Katelyn because she is not that busy and she's a freaking nurse for crying out loud. She should be there in case we need her. Plus, she's sweet. I think we need at least one more to come along...hmm...Bath Salts Mary? No. The toenail biter in the south corner with no bra and dirty hair? No. Then it hits me, what about that sweet little lunch lady, Loretta? She's so grandmotherly and warm. I'm sure she would join the party.

Me and my gang, excluding Loretta because she is not yet aware that she is in a gang, gather in the Solarium. I go over the plan which certainly can't be that difficult for these girls to remember. I may be the brains of this operation, but my goodness I've got like a million things going on and I need them to do their part. So far, it involves them waiting by the community restroom in the 200 corridor until I come and get them. It's almost five.

I nonchalantly make my way back to lunch lady land and I can smell dinner cooking. These ladies can cook! I also see a sweet little pink iced cake in a glass pan with a doily. Haha! Where did this gal find the doily? My grandma has doilies too.

"Whatcha think, sweetie? Will it do?" Loretta asks proudly.

"It's perfect! Thank you so much. But Loretta? I have to ask you one more thing."

"Oh great, I knew it," growls Gloria, "if you feed the wild animals, they'll keep coming back for more."

"She's delightful," I say.

Loretta rolls her eyes at her coworker, then looks at me and says, "What'cha need, doll?"

"This cake is for a friend. It's her birthday...well...kind of, and I thought maybe if you could sneak away for a minute you could come and sing happy birthday with some of the crazy girls. I'm trying to find recruits."

"Say no more sweetie pie. I'd be happy to come along. Gloria can manage without me for a little while. Besides, that ol' bitch gets on my last damn nerve! I ain't got too many nerves left to spare. I've got the fibromyalgia."

"Thanks so much Loretta. I'm Vada by the way."

"It's a pleasure to meet you, sugar." She turns her head towards her coworker. "Be back in a while, Gloria. I'm taking a break."

Loretta unties her apron and lickety split, she's got the cake in the air on one hand like a cocktail waitress at the casino and we are making our way down the hall towards Lauren's room. We stop and pick up the rest of our gang who are still patiently waiting in the pisser. We quiet down as we get to her door. I go to knock, but Panicky Pearl starts breathing all funny and we talk her back into normalcy.

"Now listen, sister," I say "when we are done in here you can go back to your room and scream and tear up pillows if you need to. For now, knock it the hell off and let's take turns with our crazy. Don't be so needy."

She actually listens and straightens up. I knock on the door and Lauren is standing there with red eyes.

"What is this?" she asks.

"Lauren, I'd like you to meet some of New Outlook's Center's finest wards, some of whom you know, Pearl, Jessalyn, Katelyn the Nurse, and this is Loretta."

"Okay...but...what...what are you shitheads doing here?"

"My name is not Pearl." says the panic lady. I shush her.

I count to three and we all yell, "Surprise!" We barge in and tell her we are here for her birthday party.

She is jumping up and down with excitement. Literally, it's like watching a small child. Her eyes are bright, her face has color, and her smile could reach the length of a classroom ruler.

"Oh guests! I don't know what to say, but thank you so much! Here, come over here shitheads."

We gather around her sitting area and sing the happy birthday song and everyone claps. We all eat cake, but Lauren gets the first piece because it's her special day. Her joy at this moment is almost overwhelming. She goes on to tell us what she got for her birthday, which we know is all in her mind, but who cares because she is so happy. Apparently, she got a slingshot and a set of bow and arrows. She plans on going duck hunting later and I am relieved that she is nutty because I would not want my little duck friends to be eaten by Lauren, even on her birthday.

"Sing it one more time!" she begs.

We do. In fact, we sing it three more times and she is, I believe, the happiest woman in the world, in this moment.

She goes on to share her pictures with the rest of the group and tells strange stories and we all go along with it. It is now time for us all to leave because we have schedules that we have to stick to, but she thanks us profusely for her party and as we leave she yells, "See you later, you shitheads!" She waves goodbye with a huge smile. We just made her day.

Katelyn's Relief

I walk Loretta back to the kitchen and help her catch up since we took so much of her time. After serving dinner to all the mentally deranged, I head back to my room. I am exhausted, literally, exhausted. I hear a knock on my door and in walks Katelyn, with my little white cup.

She looks at me with her perfect smile. "What just happened back there tonight was amazing. You know, that's the most I've seen Lauren smile since she's been here. Even if it was only for one day, at least she got a chance to be happy. Good job tonight, Vada. I don't know what the hell is wrong with you still, you're charts are confusing even to me, but you can't be that crazy to go and do a thing like that. Really…good job."

"It was no problem. I think that Lauren is a sweet person who needs some friends. What can I say? She's somebody's daughter. Once you have kids you start looking at everybody that way. It's kind of strange, but I hope that people will look out for my kids someday even if I'm not around. I mean, what if I died in a car accident or something? I would only hope there would be people looking out for my kids, you know?

Katelyn looks at me and smiles. Her teeth are so white! I smile back but keep my grin tight and closed. I'm getting whitening strips as soon as I get home.

"Hey Katelyn, I think I am ready to tell you what my true diagnosis is. I've dealt with this my whole life so I have learned to control it. Telling you this is hard for me, but I want you to know. You really don't know,

Katelyn? The doctors haven't spelled it all out for you?"

"No, what is it? I've tried connecting the dots, but..."

"I have multiple-personality disorder."

"No way. Oh goodness, Vada! I had no idea."

"Yeah, I know right? So what you saw tonight, well that was Gandhi...he comes out when I try to bring peace."

Katelyn looks confused. "Vada, I think you better rest for the night. I'm going to have your meds reevaluated in the morning. You are doing a great job of hiding this, if that's what you're trying to do. I have never actually met a patient with multiple personalities, but I guess that explains why you charts are so confusing. This is a first for me. I didn't know....I just..."

"Now that you know, I guess I can let you meet Paul," I say. I get up from the bed and I grab a hairbrush from the dresser. Katelyn's excited expression changes to kind of freaked out. I walk very slowly over to her and lean in taking long deep breaths. "Paul wants to come out and meet you Katelyn," I say softly. Her face is blank and she looks like she's on one of those carnival rides that spin and lift your feet off the ground and keep your whole body stiff. I think she's going to scream.

"Katelyn they are coming, they are almost here. Move Katelyn, *move*!" She looks terrified. I start galloping around the room like I'm riding a horse and yell "The British are coming! The British are coming!" I keeping galloping, hold my hairbrush up, and yell out "One if by land, two if by sea!"

Katelyn finally realizes what I'm doing and she starts yelling, "You idiot. You scared the crap out of me, Vada! I swear I almost peed in my pants. What the heck is wrong with you?"

Still laughing, "I told you what's wrong with me. I have multiple-personality disorder."

"Ha Ha! Very, very funny. You know what Vada? You need help!"

"No shit, Sherlock, look around. That's why I'm here."

We actually both laugh at that and she's not mad anymore, we are both so tired.

"Okay, Paul Revere, you are a maniac and I'm almost done with my shift so I'm leaving for the night."

"Okay, but that was rude."

"I'm off to my hotel room...because I'm homeless."

"Oh yeah Katelyn, about that...you remember my brother Heath that came to visit me?"

Her expression lights up. "Yes."

"He cleared out your apartment today and he has all of your stuff stored in a moving truck in his company parking lot."

"What are you talking about?"

"Apparently, my brother kind of has the hots for you, so when I told him your story, he was willing to help. Good thing you're a hottie. Anyways, while your little loverboy Mikey, or PinkyDick, or whatever his name is was gone today, Heath and my dad and their buddies went and got all that stuff he bought on your credit cards along with all of your furniture and everything else."

"Are you kidding me, are you seriously kidding me?"

"Heath says there are thousands of dollars' worth of electronics and some really nice golf clubs. There's even a new guitar. So Katelyn, whatever you don't want you can always sell or take back. But now he's left with nothing and you got all the stuff waiting for you to keep or sell or move right back into the apartment once he's gone."

"What do you mean once he's gone?"

"Your name is on the lease genius. Oh...and I kind of had my brother scare the piss out of him and he told him he can't come back. We just wanted to make sure he couldn't take any of his "stuff" that *you* paid for."

"Oh my God, you really are a freak show! Thank you so much Vada!" She runs over and hugs me so tight I can hardly breathe. "So he's leaving?"

"Yes. Heath and company went back later to put the fear in him. Heath said he was scared shitless. Heath's buddies are kind of, well, rugged. But you're getting a security system put in when you get back...and that's an order. Besides, from what Heath said it sounds like he's found some other girl to leech off of."

"Eww...you mean she was there?"

"Yep, but don't worry. Heath said she was really ugly with a big gooey love handles and a booger in her nose." Okay, so I was exaggerating a little.

"I knew it, but, oh well, he is her problem now!"

"So just wait a day or two, and Heath will help you move back in, okay? I wrote down his number here for you."

"Why are you doing this, Vada? Why do you care about what's happening to me? I don't understand you at all. But thank you so much."

"Oh no problem, girly. Now hand over my little pills and my schedule 'cause Paul Revere, Gandhi, and Vada are going to sleep."

"Goodnight Vada...you crazy girl."

"Good. Night. Nurse." (haha) I crack myself up.

March 7th

I wake missing my kids so much. Before I can get out of bed I have to cry my eyes out. What am I doing here? I just want to be with my babies. I've got to call Eric.

"Eric, honey...I miss you. I meant to call you before I went to sleep last night, but things got crazy here."

"That's okay. I miss you and the boys miss you too. I don't know how you do this all day Vadie. I think I'd go nuts. Oh sorry honey. I'm so sorry. I didn't mean to..."

"Oh stop it. I don't get offended anymore. You know that. Are you having Grape *Nuts* for breakfast? Or are you going *coo-coo* for Cocoa Puffs? Maybe a little *fruitcake* perhaps?"

"Vadie, you are something else. When are you coming home?"

"I'm going to find out today. I feel like my time here is almost done and I'm so ready to be back with you guys. I have two therapies and a group session today so I'm going to find out if I can be released."

"Do you want us to come see you, baby?"

"You know I do, but I wonder if we shouldn't just wait. It might make me too sad and I'm sure it will only be another day or two."

"Okay, let me know. Your mom's itching to visit. I'll see if I can hold her off."

"Alright kid. Kiss my babies and kiss your sweet scruffy self and then rub your balls and think of me."

"You know I rub my balls every time I think of you."

"That's gross."

"Yeah kinda, but anyways, I love you and call me tonight and tell me what they say."

"Okay. Wait. Hey Eric, do you really rub your balls when you think of me?'

"No, when I think of you, I think...there's my life."

"That was so fucking sweet Eric."

"Well honey, I'm a hell of a sweet guy."

After breakfast, which was delicious—cinnamon toast and chocolate milk—I head off to find Jessalyn and tell her goodbye.

I see her sitting at a table by herself looking very "modelicious" and scared shitless. She is wearing a black skirt and white top with wedged heels that she doesn't need (tall girls like to rub it in). Her make-up looks beautiful. She has a liquid-liner cat eye situation going on and it's really working for her. I know she looks good because she wants to feel confident.

"Well, my friend, do you know what to do?" I ask.

"I think I got it. It's all written out. I just hope I can go through with it."

"Sabrina will meet you there. You remember what she looks like, right? She has a white Acura and she'll be waiting in the parking lot. Trust me, it will take five minutes and you'll feel like you've known her for years. I'm going to find a way to get there, if I can. *If* for some reason I can't break out of here, just know I'll be thinking of you!"

I've set it up with Sabrina to where she'll meet Jessalyn at the party, and then she offered to just let Jess stay with her for a while until she gets a place. Sabrina is just like that. She's always willing to help anybody, even if she doesn't know them.

"Be brave. If you can't do it, it's okay; you can always kick him in the balls when no one is looking. Okay, now girl, what the hell are you waiting for?"

"Umm...my discharge papers and my ride."

"Of course that's what you are waiting on. I knew it. I knew it the whole time."

We sit there for a couple minutes until fish-lips Gerri comes and hands Jess some papers to sign. Then Rita comes and hugs her goodbye and tells her she will call her to check on her.

"Where will you be staying tonight?" Rita asks.

"A friend's house, after I leave my grandfather's birthday party."

"Okay, remember you can call me anytime for any reason."

"Thanks, Rita." And they hug goodbye.

"My ride's here it looks like," Jessalyn says and some sort of administrative person is waving her over. She walks away and doesn't look back.

Well, I guess that is that. I hope she does it for her sake. I just hope I can be there to see it!

Let's Just Move...with Dr. Lipton

"How are we today, Vada?" he says cheerfully.

"Just peachy. How are you? Sir...umm... I'd like to talk to you about going home."

"Really? Already Vada? Do you think you are ready?"

Is he kidding? Ready for what? I came. I did it. It's been a week. I participated. It wasn't what I hoped it would be. I'm ready to pack my shit, hit a *real* spa on the way home and then go back to my life...my family!

"Yes sir."

"You do realize Vada, you haven't been attending all of your sessions. It is hard to evaluate your recovery level at this point because frankly, we as your treatment team do not feel we've had your full participation."

"What? I didn't even know I had missed any."

This guy's an idiot. I'd like to take his tie and wrap it around his nuts and hang him from the door frame. Then as he would hang there by his scrotum I would smack him eight times in the face with his clipboard. It would be like a really fun piñata, except the only thing that would probably fall out may be an ink pen and a script pad. Hmm...This is sounding even better!

"For example, you were supposed to have had a session with your eating disorder group last night and you didn't show."

Well, you dummy, I was helping in the kitchen with Loretta so we could do the job you incompetent doctors are supposed to be doing with Lauren. You guys are failing because you all suck.

"Oh, I must have been confused. I had the worst headache! I'm so sorry. I'm over the bulimic thing really. I don't even think about barfing anymore, sir."

"Dr. Ames and I have a concern Vada, but we will discuss that as a group with you this evening. Now listen, I am not saying you are a prisoner and we'll keep you here for much longer, but we just need to work through a few kinks."

"Okay...I think. But just so you know I am going to check my legal rights and make sure this is all legit."

"Whatever you say, Vada. The clock is ticking, so can we just start your session?"

"Go ahead."

"I'd like to read from a blog post you wrote about...oh...a month ago. Yes, here it says, February 12th."

Doing the Mom Thing

Okay ladies,

This is a short post today, because I'm busy busy busy! But I have a question for you lovely ladies out there. Do you have those days where you feel like your house is actually shrinking? Does it ever seem like the contents inside of it may actually be growing larger? Why is it, that as the day goes on and the hour turns noon, your house's walls have grown twenty-five percent closer together? Then by five it's at fifty percent of its regular size. If your husband is an ass who doesn't come home, or a hard worker who works late, or if he's traveling, or if you're a single mom...it's practically collapsing on top of you by bedtime.

It's called cabin fever, my friends, and there is no cure for it other than getting the hell out of your house! So here's my answer to your cabin fever woes: Get the kids safely out of the house, grab a few of your precious belongings, and then burn the fucker to the ground!"

Thanks for listening,
~*V Bow*

He sets the paper down. "I'm going to stop there, Vada. You wrote this blog post and then there was an incident that took place that following day."

Oh, holy hell. I know exactly what he's talking about and I don't know why Eric had to divulge every freaking crazy thing I've done during my assessment! It was a chaotic week at my house. All the kids had taken turns being sick and I was behind on all the chores. Laundry was piling up and the whole place was cluttered. Having the kids sick for so long, we weren't able to leave the house and I was feeling so suffocated. Eric had been traveling. I hadn't had a break in what seemed like weeks. My house did seem small. My stuff seemed so big and disorganized and I just wanted out of my house. I have to admit that I kind of lost it that day. Eric was on his way home from a business trip in San Francisco. The two big boys had found some quiet time, finally, by playing Xbox and computer games. I figured I had a little bit of time, so I would straighten up the place. But I couldn't. No matter how much I picked up or cleaned, it still looked like a tornado had ripped through the house. Before I knew it, I was throwing shit in boxes and plastic tubs. The big boys even stopped their games and helped me. I'd taken the stuff out of the closets and put it in trash bags. I had my neighbor girl come sit with the kids while I ran to the store and I bought For Sale by Owner sign and stuck in my front yard. I was going to get out of there one way or another.

Needless to say, when Eric came home that evening, he was totally freaked out to see our house up for sale and our possessions practically boxed up. I had even taken the pictures off the walls. We had a long talk that night and unfortunately I had to unpack and take the sign out of the yard. I argued that I had already had a person call me for a showing, but he just hugged me and told me he would try to make my life easier. Hearing him say that he was "committed to improving my quality of life" made me fall in love with him all over again in that second. We had a great life already, three healthy children, a great marriage, great friends, but he wanted to make it even better. Yes, I know I freaked out and went a little haywire, but who doesn't have a breakdown now and then?

"Dr. Lipton, that day was a glitch. It was one moment of weakness where I may have gone a little off my rocker, but I'm better now. Besides, I'm going to wait and sell my house when property values go up."

"This is not a joke, Vada. This kind of behavior is irrational. It is not healthy. You have to realize that before you have any hope of recovery."

Really, you stupid? Do you honestly think I am proud of that? I'm not. Now shut the fuck up and let's be done.

"Dr. Lipton, I do not think this is a joke at all. I don't know what to say. I would never do something like that again. I have a headache."

I am lying about the stupid headache in hopes he'll wrap this up quickly. Dr. Lipton goes on and on like a blithering idiot asking me questions and talking about my feelings and I do my best to be polite. I let him think he is just doing his job.

Finally he shuts up and says, "Alright then, Vada. Don't forget your session this afternoon with Dr. Ames."

"I won't," I said rubbing my forehead.

"How's the headache Vada, on a scale of one to ten...and do you need a pain reliever?" he asks as I'm leaving.

I just want to leave, so I pick a number. "Eight, and no, I'll rest it off." I see him write something down and I give him a smug smile and out the door I go.

I believe the smug part came in because what had started as a light hearted therapist-patient relationship has now taken a turn towards more of a get the hell out of my face this is none of your damned business relationship. I've got more important things to do, like go back to my room and rest.

Back in the comfort of Room 109, I find a note slipped under my door. I seem to be quite the popular one.

Thank you for coming to my birthday...Love, Lauren

That makes me happy. Now, what to do? I need to check on this legal crap and see if I can just sign myself out of here, but I'm so tired for some reason and I just want to have a teeny tiny nap. Besides, it may be the last one in a long time if I am going home. My next session with Dr. Ames isn't for another two hours, so I'm just going to rest my eyes....

"Wake up Vada" I hear a voice.

"For what? Who caught my zebra?" I yell and sit straight up.

"Oh my gosh Vada! You need to lighten up on that Xanax. Vivid dreams are a common side effect." It is Katelyn. "You are late to your Ames session, now scoot. Don't get me in trouble. I'm supposed to be keeping you on track!"

I force my body out of my bed and look in the mirror. I look like Ozzy Osbourne. My hair is frizzed and all over the place, and my face looks like I need some de-puffing eye cream and a lot of make-up. I think I've been a little more stressed out than I realized. I twist my hair up in a knot on top of my head. I have no time for make-up so I just splash my face with water and flip flop my way down the hall and into the bowels of psychotherapy with Dr. Ames.

Cheating Ames

"You are late," Dr. Ames says sternly when I walk into the room.

124

"Indeed I am."

"Can you explain?"

"Of course I can explain. I was busy sleeping."

"You aren't committed to recovery, Vada."

"You aren't committed to your wife, sir."

"Excuse me? I have no idea what you are talking about." He looks guilty. I know he is, not only by what I witnessed, but just by the look on his face.

"You know *exactly* what I am talking about."

I wasn't going to say anything, but how dare he question me? I look at the picture of him and his wife on his desk. She's a middle-aged woman with dark shoulder-length hair. She looks like a regular lady. Poor lamb probably doesn't have a clue that her husband's been getting some on the desk in his office. Oh well, at least his paychecks are probably good. He glances over at the photo and his face turns into a splotchy mess. Perhaps I have struck a nerve. Who would want to sleep with this guy anyway? Not even with the lights off and bag over his head. No way! Maybe Gerri's eyes have been pulled back so tight, she can't see properly.

Seriously, though, what is wrong with me? Why am I saying this to this man? This is not at all my personality. I am not the kind of person who says things like this or gets involved in other people's business. I think maybe this place is making me mad, as in basket case mad.

"I *thought* that was you who sneez...umm...I don't know what to say. I am your doctor and we need to continue. I believe it's time to begin our session." He looks at me like he's got a rock about to be thrown at his head. He knows that I know something. This may work in my favor.

"Okay sir, let's do this."

Dr. Ames goes over the whole "find your happy place" crap and does the countdown. The next thing I know he is snapping his fingers and I'm looking at him like I just woke up naked with a guy after getting blackout drunk the night before.

"Are we done?"

"Vada, do you remember anything from hypnosis?"

"No."

"Okay then, thank you for coming and I'll talk to my colleagues this evening and we'll see where we go from here."

Okay, now I am freaking out. Why does he need to talk to his "colleagues"? I don't like the fact that he knows I heard him sexing, this does not feel right. I've got to get out of this room. I can't look at this cheating man's chins any longer.

Busting Out

I know I am supposed to meet with these idiot therapists tonight, but I really need to be there for Jessalyn and Sabrina. Surely, I'll be back in time. I've been so busy that my escape plan has been put on the back burner. But I think I have an idea and it involves a certain janitor.

I head to Room 74. He's not in there. I search up and down the halls and in the community bathrooms. I decide to check and see if he's paying a visit to Bath Salts Mary. I knock only once and bingo, I find him...getting a little afternoon delight. The sounds coming from inside the room are making my mouth fill up with warm water and I can taste puke in the back of my throat. It sounds like they are going to be done soon—for crying out loud this has to be nearing the climax. This chick sounds like she's getting a fully conscious colonoscopy, and he sounds like he is moving furniture. What the hell could they be doing in there? Mental picture...go away! I wait patiently as I realize they probably can't stop at this point. An elderly gal walks by me in a blue nightgown and slippers and growls at me. She was pleasant. Okay, I'm hearing a sound like a horse is giving birth...and now for the grand finale...Mary lets out a yelp like she just got her vaginal warts burned off with a lit cigarette. I wonder if it was as good for them as it was for me. I hate to be immature but all I can think is gonorrhea..cha cha cha.

The door finally opens and Jeremiah walks out grinning from ear to ear.

"Was Mary a dirty girl Jeremiah?' I ask. "Because you seem to have forgotten your cleaning supplies. I guess you two are back to the sex thing. Whatever."

"Oh, hey there, crazy lady. Uh...I was just saying goodbye. I'm off in thirty minutes."

"Really? Hmm...Good to know. Do you have big plans for the night?"

"Aww...not really. Just goin' home to drink beers and goin' to sleep."

"Jeremiah, I think I may have just changed your plans."

"What in the hell are you talkin 'bout?"

"You are going to get me out of here...just for a while. I need a ride and I have no one else that can do this for me." He looks at me like he thinks I am messing with him. "I'm serious. Just drop me off somewhere. It's not far, only about ten miles north and then bring me back. Only an hour tops. They won't even know I'm gone. They'll think I am resting."

He starts chewing his fingernails. This makes me want to vomit because there is probably some type of bacteria-ridden body fluid hidden under the nail beds. I'm actually pretty sure of it. Eww...

"What makes you think that I'm gonna risk my job to take you outta here?"

"Well, lover boy, if you don't...then I'll tell the administration that you are fucking Mary Weaverton and to prove it, I have a note from her saying how you guys are quite the happy couple."

"She said that?" He blushes like an idiot. I wish he'd quit licking the secretions under his fingernails.

"Yes! Now, I'll meet you by the employee exit in thirty minutes. We have to walk out like it's no big deal. If we just blend in, they'll never know."

"I guess if I have to. But just this one time, crazy lady. And only an hour." He knows he has no choice. I don't know why he's bothering with conditions.

"Okay," I say. "See ya in thirty...and knock off the crazy lady shit, I already told you once. And Jeremiah, wash your hands and then use hand sanitizer, twice!"

I go and put on the nicest pair of insane asylum fashion that I have with me. I brought along a black dress. Not a fancy dress, but one of those comfortable cotton sleeveless dresses, the kind I would wear to run errands in. It's not exactly country club material, but it will have to do. I have to wear my flip flops, because it's the best I've got. My Nike's would look a little odd. Finally, I see him coming down the hall with his goofy looking smile. He doesn't say a word. He swipes a card on an electronic panel on the side of the door. It beeps and I hear it unlock. The next thing I know...we are free; at least free to walk through the parking lot.

I can spot Jeremiah's car not because I have ever seen or heard what he drives, but because it looks like Jeremiah, if he were a car. Let me explain. It's an early 80's white Pontiac station wagon with a red hood and red and orange flames on both sides. The windows are already rolled down and there is a bumper sticker that reads, "Balls." I can't help but laugh on the inside, because it just works for him. I walk around to the passenger side and he immediately stops me.

"Uhh...sorry 'bout that, but that door got busted and it don't open, 'fraid you gonna have to crawl through my side."

Charming. I crawl through and am already regretting my choice of chauffeur. The car reeks of cigarette smoke and the seats are vinyl and sticky. I try my best not to touch anything with my hands and crawl in as quickly as I can, so that I can breathe out the open window. There is a smell coming from the back seat. It's either a dead body or rotten meat of some kind. Probably a dead body. I try to be nice and hope I am wrong.

"Nice car," I say. "You know where we are headed?"

"Uh…thanks and not a damn clue, lady."

"Okay, it's the Bristol Glenn Country Club just north of here."

"Oh yep, I know where that is. My twin brother used to caddie there."

Oh my! There are two of these mutants. I can't imagine another Jeremiah. But he's out there somewhere, probably just mixing up more stupid into the world. We are on our way and I glance in the mirror on the visor and put on some lip gloss and fix my hair. I am going to a country club after all.

It doesn't take long and I am dropped off in style, super awesome station wagon-valet style. I see Sabrina's car in the parking lot, which is a huge relief. I tell my driver to be back to get me in an hour. He agrees. I walk in nervous, but I'm glad I made it. It's a beautiful swanky place with cherry wood paneling and circular tables with white tablecloths. There is a slide show playing and pictures are flying across the screen to some old time songs I am not familiar with. I spot the head table where the old man sits as the guest of honor. He looks larger than I expected and very "with it." He sure doesn't look ninety to me. He's no spring chicken, but doesn't look like he just crawled out of a grave or anything. Jessalyn and Sabrina are sitting at a round table just to the left. I am not even kind of dressed appropriately, but what do you do?

The girls see me and immediately smile and wave. I wish I looked as cute as Sabrina in her flowy green top and brown pants, and Jessalyn, who is still rocking her black and white skirt and top combo. They can't believe I actually made it and truthfully, I can't either. I am officially an escapee from the psych ward. They are both so excited to see me, and I am glad for that. I know it's a nervous night for Jessalyn. I'm grateful to Sabrina for coming to meet a total stranger for moral support. But that's kind of our rule. Any friend of hers is a friend of mine and vice versa. That is...unless the friend tries to take either one of our places and then we ditch the bitch.

"May as well eat something while the food's out," Jessalyn says. "May as well grab a cocktail too. You are going to need one."

I guess I may as well. It's a buffet dinner set up with all sorts of different food. Chicken spiedini, some sort of meatballs, pastas and sauces, dips, bread, salads, desserts, and they seem to all end up somewhere on my plate, except the red sauce. Then I head to the bar for a vodka&7 and go back and sit down with the girls. I notice that Jessalyn is not eating, but she does have a glass of red wine. She probably *is* going to need it. We are at a table set for eight people, but it's just the three of us plus two men in brown suits who look like they must be old friends of Jessalyn's grandfather. They are watching the slideshow and sipping on drinks. They are both old and have kind-looking faces. I bet they have lots of grandkids and would be appalled to know what their dear old friend did to one of his own. I look around the room and notice a banner that reads, "Happy Birthday Wallace!" There is also a stand with a guest book that I do not plan on signing.

Many of the guests are finishing dinner and are up mingling and making small talk. This is quite a nice party actually. By the looks of this group, old man Wallace has many friends and lots of family. The one guest that strikes my fancy is a very drunk old lady on a Hover Round Scooter. I've seen her run into two tables already and she keeps yelling out, "Play Brickhouse!" I like her. What a fun gal. She has short gray hair that is sprayed into a perfect sphere. She is rocking a gold dress with white lace-up orthopedic shoes. She's like an elderly fashionista on wheels. She keeps riding her scooter up to the bar and says, "One more to keep me young!" That will be me someday. I just know it. Oh damn...she just ran over a woman's toe. That had to hurt. It's a good thing there are no cops here, or she would get a DUI on that scooter.

There are not many children here that I can see, but I do see one little girl in a cream dress with black polka-dots, and she is hanging on her mother's leg. My mother antennae suddenly go up and I can't help but keep my eye on her and make sure she doesn't leave my sight with a pedophile in the room.

"Tell me, who is who," I say to Jessalyn, "at least the important people."

"Okay, see that older lady over there with the gray roots and reddish hair? That's my aunt who raised me after my mother died. Her name is Katherine. Over in the corner, the pretty girl with the man candy is my cousin Erin, Katherine's daughter and that is her daughter, Maggie." I realize she is talking about the little girl in polka-dots.

"How old is your cousin? Were you raised in the same house together?"

"She's five years older than me, and yes we were raised together with my grandfather and my aunt after my mom died. We were never that close. She was always just interested in boys and just enough older than me that we had nothing in common. She moved out when she was seventeen, she got pregnant with a son, but lost custody of that child. Who knows where

131

he is now…so sad. See that guy she's with? That's not Maggie's father. She doesn't even know who the father is…"

I notice that Jessalyn's eyes are not with us, she's off in deep thought somewhere.

'Well," she says "I'll go get us some more drinks!" She quickly trots off to the bar leaving me and Sabrina sitting with our hot dates in the brown suits. I claim dibs on the one with the curly mustache.

"Holy crap, Vadie, what the hell have you gotten us into?" Sabrina is giving me that look.

"I don't know, but thank you for coming bestie," I say.

"I think she's going to chicken out."

"So what if she does," I say, "at least she tried."

Jessalyn comes over and drops off more drinks and sits down. Sabrina and I quiet down and a voice comes over a microphone. It's her aunt, Katherine.

"Good evening everyone." The music is cut and the room is silent. "I would like to thank you all for coming out tonight to celebrate this wonderful occasion. Today as you know marks the ninetieth birthday of my amazing beloved father, Wallace Dickey." Wallace sits in his chair soaking up the attention like a sponge.

Sabrina and I immediately shoot each other a look. Is his last name seriously Dickey? Jessalyn starts laughing when she sees us looking at each other and the brown-suited silver foxes glare at us like we are hoodlums. We are.

"As you know, my father Wallace is a war veteran, a member of the Rivergate Society for a Greener Community, an entrepreneur, a retired school board member, (I gasp) a political activist, and the most gentle and kind-hearted man I have ever known. And as many of you know he lost a daughter many years ago and found the strength in his heart to help me raise his orphaned granddaughter. He's a true hero."

(applause)

I swallow the rest of my drink. I can't believe that this woman is saying this into a microphone, like Jessalyn is not sitting in the room. Many guests glance at our table and nod, as if oh yes, this burden on him sitting here at this table should entitle him to such praise. What a joke.

Katherine keeps going as if she has just introduced the president. "Happy Birthday to you, sweet Daddy. I will always love you and I hope we are here to celebrate twenty more birthdays for you." She raises her glass and so does the rest of the room. I look at Jess, to see her reaction but she is back at the bar ordering another round. If this man is still celebrating another birthday in twenty years I'm afraid I'll have to attend along with the people from the *Guinness Book of World Records*.

Katherine, so proud of herself, introduces several people who also come up and sing old man Wallace's praises. We are sipping on our drinks I think we are all feeling a wee bit tipsy. Katherine takes back the microphone.

"I know that there is one more person here, who would like to say something about her grandfather. The person who was saved by him most of all. The person who really owes him her very life right now. Jessalyn, I would like you to come and say a few words…to your grandfather about what he means to you."

Oh God. This wasn't what was supposed to happen. We had a different plan. The plan was going to be leaving notes at the end of the party to the people she thought should know the truth. She is going to crack. How dare this woman put her up to this! Jessalyn looks at me surprised.

"You don't have to go up there," I say.

She suddenly gets a vixen-like smile on her face and says "Oh, yes I do."

Sabrina and I sit and watch as she takes her red wine up to the podium and adjusts the microphone. I watch Wallace's eyes on her and I see what she means about the threatening look she told me about. His face has changed from an old man to a villain in a storybook, kind of like that guy from *Poltergeist*. He almost looks evil. She looks down at the floor and then forces her eyes to the crowd.

"Hello everyone. I am the one who owes my life to this man. After the death of my mother, he and my aunt took me in. They let me eat and sleep and they even gave me a bed. Can you imagine that? Can you imagine a little orphaned girl all scared and alone…being taken in by her very own family? He is a hero, just like you all say. I mean without him I wouldn't be where I am today…just released from rehab."

The crowd is confused; almost as if they aren't sure they heard this right. People are looking at each other and the tension in the room is growing as thick as the bush of Bath Salts Mary.

"I mean, why didn't they just let me starve? Well, don't worry everyone…I'm taking care of that now. Can't you see that for yourselves?" Jessalyn lifts up her shirt to just underneath her bra revealing protruding hip bones and ribs. A gasp fills the room. Katherine stands up and starts to interrupt, but is quickly shut down by her daughter Erin. Erin then whispers to her boyfriend to take Maggie outside. He puts her on his shoulders and they bounce out the door.

"So Katherine, first I would like to thank *you*, for not letting me physically die. I was already dead enough on the inside. All those nights you pretended not to notice him coming into my room. You pretended not to notice what was going on right in front of your face. You let him do it!"

Jessalyn is now shouting and tears are falling down her face. She turns her glare toward Wallace. "My mother should have killed *you* instead of herself. So go ahead and toast to your hero everyone, but while you're at it take a look at his troubled Granddaughter. I'm sure everyone has always wondered why dear old Wallace's granddaughter has so many problems. Why she doesn't come to visit him? Why doesn't she call him once in a while, especially on holidays? Well, I'm here now aren't I? Yes I am...so here's to you." She raises her glass. "Happy birthday motherfucker." Jessalyn throws her glass down to the floor and it shatters. The room is in total shock. She looks at me and Sabrina and we know it's best to follow her right out the door. I look around at the stunned guests and throw up a wave and say "goodbye." I then look at Wallace and say "Happy Birthday." Oh my God that was so awkward. Why would I say goodbye? Why would I wish him a happy birthday? I'm such an idiot. I clearly can't handle awkward situations.

As we are walking out I hear the old woman on the scooter reversing her cart. I know this because I can hear the beeping noise. I then hear her start cussing out Katherine and Wallace. I can't make out exactly what she said, but I hear enough to know she used the words "ashamed of yourself" and "piss on your grave." I knew I liked her.

Once we are in the parking lot, Jessalyn sees Maggie and Erin's boyfriend throwing rocks onto the golf course. Jessalyn runs over to Maggie and gives her a big bear hug and kisses her face. Then she runs toward Sabrina's car and we follow, still stunned. A voice in the distance is yelling "Wait!" It is Erin.

She catches up about ten feet away from the car and her eyes are full and red. "I'm sorry I didn't help you back then," she says. "I was young and stupid and I trusted my mother's choices. I was wrong Jess...I hope someday you can forgive me."

"I do forgive you, Erin," she says. "Just take care of Maggie and never, *ever* let anything happen to her."

135

"I won't."

We get in the car and drive off. Jessalyn busts out laughing. "Did you see the look on his face? Did you see Katherine? I can't believe I did that. That was priceless! I bet he shit in his grandpa diaper!"

I seriously am speechless. I don't know what to say and I know Sabrina is about to lose it. I can only imagine what she must be thinking.

"I feel like I am free! I feel like I have had chains on me my whole life, and now they are gone. I feel like now...I'm not living a lie anymore."

"Well," I say, "that's sensational!"

"Sensational?" Jessalyn asks. "Who the hell uses the word sensational?"

"I'm glad at this point, Jess, that you are interested in the particular choice of words that I am using. For crying out loud, after what just happened at the bash, I think right now we should really be focusing on my word choices!"

Girl's Night Out

"Let's celebrate!" Jessalyn yells.

"Why not?" agrees Sabrina.

"Umm, ladies...I think I forgot my ride was supposed to pick me up like an hour ago!" Oh crap! I really did forget. Jeremiah must have been waiting outside and I didn't pay an ounce of attention to the time. Well, the therapy panel's going to shit a brick.

"Nothing we can do now. Let's go get one drink, just one, and we'll take you back to the nuthouse."

"Might as well," I say and throw my hands up. Sabrina steps on the gas and we head down the road to an old biker bar called Carl's. She passes out smokes and I didn't know Jessalyn smoked, but apparently we all do now, at least for tonight. I know she chooses this bar because no one here would ever recognize us, unless there are some bad-ass moms in the kids' school that I just don't know about. All I know is that neither Sabrina nor I have ever been here. I doubt Jessalyn has either. It doesn't seem to be a hangout for models. It's just one of those bars you drive past and don't notice.

We walk in and the place is not crowded for a Friday night, at least I would assume this bar at least gets some sort of crowd on the weekends. There is a row of pool tables occupied by some ZZ Top looking guys and a few ladies in short skirts and dreadfully high heels. It is dark and smoky and has a 70's vibe with vintage red shade lights hanging from the ceiling. I realize we stand out like three sore thumbs, but I've had enough to drink that I really don't care. We find an empty table and plop down like turds in a punchbowl. A bleach blonde waitress who looks like she's been ridden slick, walks over and asks what we "little girls" want to drink.

"Three tequila shots!" Jessalyn yells out.

"Right," says the waitress, like she thinks it's so cute that we are trying to be big bad tequila drinkers.

I know this is a bad idea. First of all, I am a puker when I drink. Second of all, tequila makes me crazy. Kind of ironic isn't it? What the hell. I'm already a fugitive. I may as well act like one. After our shots arrive staring us in the face like, "what now bitches?" Jessalyn pours our salt and raises her glass.

"Here's to one sick and twisted anorexic, one mentally messed up mommy, and one chick who's up for anything…and…to new friends."

I raise my glass. It dawns on me that we will probably stay friends.

People don't just go through these kinds of experiences and then never see each other again. We suck our limes and before I know it, I can't really remember how many we've had. All I know is that there is music playing on the jukebox and when you combine music and tequila, asses start shaking. I'm not sure if there is a dance floor but we seem to have decided that there is. We even push tables back to make some room. Not only are we dancing, but so is the waitress who is now chugging a beer, and we seem to have attracted some very hairy- and scary-looking men who are twirling us around to the sounds of Poison. I do believe I am a bit wasted, Sabrina is looking trashed, and ninety-pound Jessalyn appears to be drunk, but otherwise getting along quite swimmingly.

The next thing I know, we are on the bar and we are using every square foot of it as our stage. Apparently we are quite a fun bunch and so is the company we are keeping. The music is blaring. Jessalyn is getting dollar bills thrown at her and Sabrina is double fisting her beers and yelling "Play some Kid Rock!" What would the other room moms think? Can you imagine? Here's the mom providing crafts and games for all the school holiday parties...drunk, dancing, and smoking on a bar with bikers all around. We are acting like spring breakers in Cancun. A beefy gentleman grants Sabrina's request for Kid Rock and the three of us women act like we won the lottery. You must bear in mind that I drive a mini-van. Our beer bottle microphones and screaming over the music and shenanigans are not my typical Friday night activities. I'm so wasted that it just doesn't matter. We are dancing with moves we didn't even know we had.

The next thing I know, I hear a thud, and see the floor. I seem to have fallen off the damned bar, flat on my face. Then I see blood. I think it's my nose. I can't really feel it. A mob of beards and bandanas flock to my side and pull me up. The music stops. Okay, I'm embarrassed. Sabrina and Jessalyn are just frozen looking down at me. A short bald guy hands me a napkin for my nose. I pinch it to stop the bleeding. Have you ever had an entire bar staring at you at the same time in silence? I put the napkin down on a table, throw my arms up and yell, "ROCK AND ROLL BITCHES!"

Applause, applause, and more applause. The music starts again and

I'm back on the bar acting like a fool. It's like nothing ever happened. Song after song, beer after beer we finally start to wear down. We dance and drink until we can no longer speak proper English. We are so drunk that our dancing has turned into just waving our arms like one of those blow-up critters they put up in front of car dealerships.

"Last call for alcohol!" the bartender hollers over the music, which is now KISS.

"What the hell time is it?" I ask.

Sabrina yanks out her cell phone from her purse. "One forty-five," she yells.

"Oh my freaking bloody hell!" I yell. "I'm in so much trouble! When did it get so late?"

Sabrina decides to call a cab, which is really the only smart decision we make all night long. A delicious looking man, who I think may have fleas and a rash under his beard, takes care of our tab. Our cab driver looks at us suspiciously and then shrugs his shoulders when I tell him the first stop is the New Outlook Center. I can't even imagine what he must be thinking, and being so drunk I find the whole thing quite hilarious. It's no time at all before our Deluxi-Cab pulls into the parking lot and the dimmed lights inside suggest that all the crazies have been sedated and are sleeping peacefully in the safe confines of the mental ward. The driver stops and I get out on the curb. I thank the girls for a fun night. We all hug goodbye and I promise to call them and let them know when I am going home.

I find myself standing on the curb and watching them drive off. I am in a drunken stupor and I realize that I am barefoot and must have left my flip flops in the cab. That's a problem when I drink. First of all, I would normally never take off my shoes off in a cab of all places. Plus, I can never remember what I am doing. Then it hits me…how the hell am I going to get inside? What was I thinking? I can't just walk in the front door and tell security I had a real nice time at Carl's. I should be slapped. I don't know what is wrong with my brain. I had this big grand plan to sneak out of here and I thought it went quite well, but I never even thought about getting back in. I immediately panic. What if they can see me? What if they notice I am missing and have put a crappy picture of me on the news and the whole state is looking for Ben, Max, and Jordan's mom…escaped psychiatric patient, considered dangerous. Fan-freaking-tastic. This is going to be great for me at my sons' baseball games. I can just see the mom's chatting on the bleachers together taking turns catching glimpses of me without being too obvious. No one will invite my kids to birthday parties. Who wants their kids hanging out with "that one lady's" kids? "That one lady" who was on the news…"that one lady" who was in the mental ward. They'll never let their kids come over for play dates in fear that their children may be duct-taped to the wall and covered with mayonnaise. There's no telling what could happen at "that one lady's" house. I am pacing around like a total freak show and I notice the chain link fence that begins on the side of the building. I brace myself because I know I'm going to have to climb that fucker.

The night air is warmer than I thought it would be and I realize I'm sweating. Warm water starts to fill my mouth and I know I'm going to hurl. I run over to the nearest bush by the fence and puke my guts out. I feel much better. There are thick trees lining the fence and I search for a spot where I can get underneath the branches. There it is, a little clearing, and I duck down through the tangled leaves and take a grip on the metal. This is not going to be fun barefoot. This fence has got to be at least eight foot high. Did I mention I am only five foot high? I start to make the climb. I'm so drunkie and so wobbly, but I am doing quite well. I am up about a foot off the ground and I am not even bleeding yet. I keep the climbing going and am pleasantly surprised at how good I am at this. I would never be able to do this sober. I make it to the top and although it is dark and I am covered by tree branches, I decide to bear all my weight on my right arm and swing my body over. Okay…here goes nothing. As I press down with my right hand to make the swing I feel an insane and unnatural sensation spread throughout my wrist. It's wet. My legs have gone forward, but my feet aren't on the ground. They are catching on the fence and my hand is stuck. My hand is stuck in motherfucking barbed wire and blood is streaming everywhere. I realize that my dress is torn, my ass cheeks are bleeding and I'm pretty sure I am cut up all down my legs. Well ain't this a bitch? What a way to die.

I can imagine the conversation the grief counselors have with my kids. Your mother died climbing a barbed wire fence children...oh and her blood alcohol level was four times the legal limit...oh...and she was in the mental ward. This is not good. I realize that if I was sober it would hurt a lot worse, so I am thankful for my bad choices...kind of. I decide that it's best to just bleed out and not make too much of a mess. My eyes can't stay open, and I feel myself being lifted up, lifted up to a better place.

March 8th

My trip to heaven was cut short. When I opened my eyes to the bright light, I expected to see the Lord, but instead it was a fluorescent light and a bug was caught in it. I was staring at the ceiling in a hospital emergency room. The aftermath...it's all coming back to me. Country club, Jessalyn, Sabrina, dancing, bar, cab, fence...Oh my God the fence! Someone must have found me. Where the hell are the doctors? I'm so hung over already and I don't even know if its morning. The door opens and in walks a super young and yummy looking doctor. He's tall, clean cut, black hair, blue eyes that I should not look into, and green scrubs. How does this guy make scrubs look so good? I bet he thinks that I'm a dish as well. I can only imagine the troll I would see if I looked in the mirror. I can feel my eyes are burning and watery and I know my hair probably looks like Charles Manson's. I bet I smell good too, probably like a hobo. I bet he wants a piece of this.

"Vada, glad you are awake. I'm coming to check your dressings."

My dressings...oh no. I know I cut up my butt. Is he going to look at my butt?

"You took quite a beating, you poor thing."

I did? What does he mean? I look at him clueless.

"When the triage nurse was questioning you about your injuries you stated that you were attacked by two women named Dorothy and Blanche. You described them as elderly and wearing floral dresses with shoulder pads. You didn't want to file a police report."

Oh what is the hell is wrong with me? Why would I say that? I was so drunk I don't remember anything after the fence. I put a hand over my face and feel a burning sensation in my fingers.

"I would try to keep that still. You have quite a few stitches in that

142

left hand and you need to rest it as much as possible. You also have several stitches in your lower back, left leg, and your left buttock."

Oh my buttock. Why did he have to say buttock? I hate that word. It's so fleshy sounding and gross. It makes me think of an Easter ham. He walks to the other side of the bed and has me lean over to get a better glimpse of my buttock. He lifts up the sheet and I realize I am terribly tensed up from being nervous. So he probably sees the attractive looking form of two cheeks tightly clinched like they are holding on to a pencil. I am further mortified as he confirms my fear of the cheek-squeeze when he says, "Just relax." I relax my poor injured buttocks and he gets a good look of my rear and then lays the sheet back over me. He investigates my other sutured injuries and seems satisfied.

"You're lucky, you know," he says and looks me in the eye, "most of my patients who are beat up by the Golden Girls are in much worse shape than you are." He winks and walks out of the room leaving the blue curtain waving behind him.

Later that day, after being discharged from Rivergate Memorial Hospital with a splitting headache, a lot of stitches, and a prescription for painkillers, I am transported back to the looney bin by none other than Gerri the coveting botox-queen nurse and a driver named Eli who seems to find me interesting. The digital clock on the car radio says it is one thirty. I must have slept a good-while in the emergency room. Gerri tells me that I was found by a security guard around three thirty in the morning. How did they not miss me until three thirty in the morning? Some top notch joint they must be running here to be missing a patient for that long and not notice! I'd like to speak to someone about that. I am sore and tired and am *never* drinking again as long as I live. I am such an idiot. So far, no one has brought up the fact that I was wasted. Someone has to be covering for me, but who? I need to find out what happened, but Gerri immediately walks me to my room and gives me my pain meds. She tells me to rest and that she has called my husband and he is coming up to check on me. She'll let me know when he gets here. I realize that Katelyn must have the day off and I'm stuck with this little home-wrecker of a nurse probably for the rest of the day. I'm thankful that Eric is coming, although I have no idea what I am going to tell him. The truth would sound insane and I can't think of a good lie. I am just going to play this one by ear. But for now, I am sore and am just going to shut my eyes. The pain medicine is making my skin itch and the sooner I get to sleep, the sooner I can wake up and see Eric.

I wake up to a knock at the door. It opens and in walks Dr. Ames with Eric trailing right behind him. Dr. Ames looks pissy and is wearing clothes that seem way too casual for him. Although still not frumpy, a collared black shirt and khaki pants is not his usual attire. Eric looks so worried. His hair is a mess and he needs to shave, but looks pretty good when he gets all homeless looking. He calls it his mountain man look. He has on jeans and a crew neck blue and gray striped long-sleeved shirt. It's wrinkled. The iron must not work when I am not home. I try to sit up to greet him but the painkillers have not taken all the pain away. I wince. Eric rushes over and kisses my forehead.

"Stay where you are, don't get up." says Dr. Ames. "We normally do not let visitors into patient rooms, but in this particular case I am willing to make an exception. I thought I would bring your husband down here personally."

"Thank you, Dr. Ames." I say and I mean it. Eric is holding my non-injured hand but stays quiet. I hope he's not mad. He seems more concerned than angry.

"You see, Mr. Bower, your wife sustained injuries last night on the grounds sometime in the middle of the night. We have had Vada on a regimen of medications designed for her needs specifically. One of those medications is a sleeping pill, which we have found highly effective in patients like Vada. Side effects like this are extremely rare, but in this case we believe that Vada was sleep-walking and during this episode, attempted to climb the fence. I have already explained to you her injuries and they are minor, however as you can see, your wife had a pretty tough fall. That fence was topped with barbed wire for security reasons. She did receive a

144

tetanus shot at the hospital as well as antibiotics and medication for the pain. The hospital found her well enough to release her to us, so we will make sure she gets what she needs."

What the hell is this rubbish that is spewing out of this mad man's mouth? I'm not complaining. It's much better than the real story, which would leave me with a lot of explaining, but does he really think this is what happened? I am so confused, but kind of in a good way. I wasn't even here to take the sleeping pill last night.

Eric looks kind of pissed. "It sounds to me, Dr. Ames, that there is some negligence on the part of this hospital. How could you let a patient sleep walk outside? Don't you lock the doors? I would think you would have security in place so that someone couldn't just go in and out in the middle of the day, let alone in the middle of the night."

I look back at Dr. Ames.

"Yes Mr. Bower. I understand your concerns and we will be reviewing the security tapes to find out exactly what happened. I am assuming one of the staff must have made a terrible mistake and we will deal with that directly when we find out who was at fault."

I look at Eric.

"Well, I should hope so. I don't want to be rude or anything but this sounds like someone really screwed up. I'm just glad she's okay."

That's Eric, always trying not to be rude. If this story wasn't so blatantly false I would be offended that he wasn't angrier. But I'm just going to lay here and see how this plays out.

"Mr. Bower, I assure you that this will be corrected and we will cover the cost of all medical bills incurred from this incident. The important thing now is that Vada is patched up and resting and I assure you she is in good hands and nothing like this will ever happen again." Now Dr. Ames is looking at me, looking at me funny, actually. I look away like a shamed child. "I'll leave the two of you alone now, just ring the front desk and I'll have someone walk you out when you are ready."

"Dr. Ames, do you think Vada could just come home? Is she ready?"

"Actually, no I don't. She has been here a week. I hardly think it's time and neither do my colleagues."

Now I am pissed. "What?!" I yell. "I am so ready. I'm done with this place. You said that you were going to get me out of here."

"Vada, I said I would review it with the other doctors and we would have discussed it last night, had you not had that awful headache..."

He looks at me and raises an eyebrow suggestively.

"Oh yes, I had an awful headache." I lie, but I'm not sure why. He's definitely the one covering for me.

"However, I cannot in good faith discharge you from here in your current condition. We need to discuss after care treatment and any medication changes that need to be made. Give me until tomorrow. Get some rest. I have an intensive session planned tomorrow if you are feeling well enough and I think it will enlighten you."

Eric kisses my face. "At least you can rest here. If you come home, the kids will be all over you. At least one more day won't hurt. Can you do that, honey?"

"Oh fine!" I growl.

"Thank you for being patient, Vada. We can't be fixed overnight." He walks out and shuts the big creaky door behind him.

Eric fills me in on the kids and tells me who's being naughty and

146

who's being nice. I miss them and I am so ready to go home. I tell Eric about some of the crazies I've befriended and about some of my sessions. We spend some time just sitting together and holding hands. It makes me really appreciate having him. He puts up with all my crap, both good and bad. After an hour, he has to go and I am starving. He kisses me goodbye and tells me he'll check on me tomorrow. He promises I will be home soon. I'm starting to wonder if that is true. I know I will eventually tell Eric about what really happened last night. This is just not the time...or the place.

Right when I think he's going to walk out the door, the inevitable happens. Eric gives me that look. You know the one I'm talking about. I am so reluctant, but considering the circumstances, I feel like it's the very least I could do. I mean for the love of Peter, Paul, and Mary, he has put up with me and taken care of my babies for this long. I try the whole "yank 'em down and go to it" thing but he wants to be all romantic. He lays my head on the bed and softly and slowly brushes back my hair with his fingers. He gives me a look again, which after seven years of marriage, I know means he wants to go downstairs. It's not that he is not good at it. In fact, I do believe that if tampering with lady bits was an Olympic sport he would get a gold medal, it's just that I'm not mentally or physically prepared for him to go downstairs at this time. First of all, they don't let nuts have razors. Secondly, I haven't showered since yesterday.

"Eric, I haven't showered since yesterday...what is wrong with you?"

"I don't care Vada, you're not on your period or anything." He's right, at least that was over. They are awful but don't last long. "If you really want to take a shower, then let me go with you."

Oh fiddly dee. I hate the sex in the shower thing. It's so awkward and I am so short that water gets in my eyes and then my contacts slip out and then I'm blind and blinking all while being thrusted into under running water, which happens to always find a way to hit nothing but my face so I am always freezing and bitching the whole time. Not sexy to me. Not sexy at all. Short girls are not built for shower sex, unless they are with a really short man.

"You know what? Let's just do a washcloth and soap situation...since I really am sore and I would like to be clean. There's stuff in the bathroom. Could you just clean me up?"

Eric looks at me like I am the lamest chick ever and he may be right, but dammit I fell off a bar and then a damned fence for crying out loud. He can take care of me. I'll eventually let him put it in, but he could at least clean me up first. I have kind of an issue with body fluid and cleanliness...if you haven't noticed. I don't like wet things. Take what you will from that bit of information, but it's true. Eric disappears into the bathroom and comes back with towels and a few paper cups full of warm soapy water. He undresses me and I think that he is actually finding this kind of hot. I probably would too if it wasn't for all the stitches. But oh well. He lays towels all around me and rubs me with warm washcloths. It actually feels really good and it's sweet because he's so careful around my sore spots. He gets two wash cloths and rubs them from my stomach with two hands up to my boobies. He must think my boobies are really dirty because he seems to be cleaning them very thoroughly.

"You're going to pop the implants there buddy if you scrub those any harder!" I say.

"Oh, sorry. Geez, I paid for them and I haven't seen them in so long."

"Well, they are clean now, move along. I don't want anyone walking in here and catching us being all naked and stuff."

"It's just like at home isn't it...you haven't taken your eyes off that door."

"Really Eric, would you not be embarrassed at all if a nurse or a doctor came in to check on me right now?"

"No. I wouldn't," he says. "I'd be like, hey man, I got a thing for the crazy girls, now get outta here unless you wanna watch the rodeo queen defend her title."

"Oh you are so gross, and I'm hurt you idiot, so there will be no rodeo in here today. Now give me that damn washcloth and let me finish cleaning up and then you can put it in me real quick, but hurry up because I know someone's going to come to the door."

As per usual, Eric does what he is told, even though it's not *his* way. It's not that I don't find him hot, but my pain meds are making me itch and I am so paranoid about that door opening, that I'm just hoping this goes quick. It's also not the best feeling considering I have to get on all fours (two knees and two elbows since my hand hurts) because it's the only position my stitches won't rub. I can't really move so I just have to stay still and take it like a little mutt dog. I probably look like one too, because I'm trying to scratch my face with my teeth and I'm wincing from the pain of these injuries. I'm glad he cannot see my face. I probably look like I have rabies. Poor Eric can't even screw his wife like a normal person. I always have to make everything so difficult. Why is this taking him so long? I know someone's going to walk in that door. My butt cheek hurts. This doggie-style thing is not working for me. We need to get this show on the road.

"Hurry up baby," I say.

"I'm trying."

"Think about boobies," I say, "and butts!"

"Shut up. Don't make me laugh, you are breaking my concentration."

"I'm not making you laugh. I'm serious...hurry up and do whatever it takes. Think about someone else for pity's sake. How about...oh...I don't know..."

"You're not helping. Quit talking normally. Talk like we are having

149

sex."

"Umm...okay. How is the sex going there, dear? This a fine day for having sex, ain't it? I'm sure glad we are doing the sex."

"Oh Vada just shut the hell up! I'm almost done. You obviously aren't into this."

"Yes I am! You are rude. Why would you say that? I'm in the hospital you know?"

"Vada...shhh...just shut up."

"Oh fucking fine...boobs and butts and big floppy nipples!"

Eric finally finishes. "Seriously Vada, what is wrong with you?" But then he pulls me up and kisses me. It was a real kiss, one that wasn't a joke. Now I kind of feel bad. I think maybe I may have ruined that whole sex vibe thing. Oh well, it's over now. Too late!

"It was the big floppy nipples comment I made that turned you on wasn't it?" I ask, laughing.

"I wasn't even listening to you, but if you said that, then no. I'm not into big and floppy anything, but thanks for trying."

Eric gets dressed, and then helps me get dressed and lo and behold we hear a knock at the door and in walks Dr. Ames.

"Just wanted to check on you, Vada. I didn't know your husband was still here."

"He was just leaving. Maybe you could call for someone to walk him out?"

"Yes, of course," says Dr. Ames. He picks up the room phone and pages a nurse. Wanda, the nurse who seems to be excited for the apocalypse, comes in to walk him out. Eric gives me one last kiss goodbye and says he'll hopefully see me at home tomorrow. I love him.

This is the part I did not want to happen. Dr. Ames is standing there all stout and splotchy and he looks nervous. Why the hell is he nervous? I'm the one who snuck out, got trashed, and ended up in the hospital from climbing a fence.

"Vada," he says in a more serious tone than I would like "I would like to say this only once and then you and I shall never speak of this again. I realize you are aware of my relationship with Gerri. It was wrong. My wife and I have been going through marital problems and I made some very poor choices during a period of weakness. I am ashamed and embarrassed of the affair. I have a plan for change. Gerri and I have decided to end our relationship and it is now strictly professional. Does anyone else know about this?"

I shake my head no.

"Very good. Now let's keep it that way. I will report your incident last night in the way I described it to your husband. I have had the security tapes destroyed and told the staff that I went to check them and they were blacked out...recording error, if you will. I told the staff you were resting with a headache and that is why you failed to report to your session. Do you understand what I mean, Vada?"

"You mean if I keep your secret, you'll keep my secret?"

"Precisely. After I leave this room, I am your doctor, you are my patient...and none of this ever happened. Gerri is aware of course, as she had to come and get you, but like I said, all that is in the past."

"I like the way you think, doc." I smile as sweet as cherry pie. "It's all forgotten!"

"Thank you, Mrs. Bower." Ooh...I'm Mrs. Bower now.

"No sweat...but Dr. Ames, I really am ready to go home."

"Yes, I know. We'll work on that, just let us work with you tomorrow and we'll see what we can do about that, okay? If I let you go now, things would look suspicious. Bear with me and I will see what can be done. You must be patient."

"Okay."

"Now you rest the remainder of the evening. Dinner will be on its way soon and should you need medical attention, please ring your nurse. We will need to stay on top of your pain medications and I don't want you getting up tonight, unless it's to use the restroom. You should feel better sooner if you get some rest."

"You got it, Dr. Ames."

Dinner comes and I am famished. I would really eat anything, but this is not what I would have picked. It is some kind of cheese and chicken situation with vegetables. What I would really like is a burger and fries. I eat this nonsense anyways and it's not that bad. I fill my belly and drink a huge glass of iced tea. I lay there tired and satisfied thinking of all the things I am looking forward to when I get home. But my stomach lurches. My much needed dinner is unfortunately taking a turn for the worse and I feel like I am going to hurl. I try to get up and make it to the bathroom, but my sore body will not get me there fast enough. I grab my plate and lean off my bed and try to hit the target. It splashes off the plate and onto the floor. Super. Now I need to clean up this vomit, but I do feel much better. I am not even considering going all the way to the bathroom to get a towel, so I take off my sweatshirt (I have a tank top underneath) wipe it up, and toss it in the hamper across the room. I'm impressed by that shot...nothing but net. I do realize what I have done just there is quite gross, but after having three boys, you learn that your shirts can be used for many purposes, like wiping noses and catching spit-up. So long as it's cleaned up right away, I can handle it. I hide the plate under my bed. I just can't get up right now.

I lay there, realizing that I really need to get back to my life. I need to update my blog. Most importantly, I need to be parenting my children. My mind is racing and I have so much guilt that it makes me want to jump out of my skin. I am so relieved when Katelyn walks in. She's looking beautifully perfect as always and seems like she is trying to hide a smile.

"What the hell happened to you? No...I don't want to know. Yes I do, and I have your meds. So start talking."

I fill her in on what happened with the sneak out and swear her to secrecy. I leave out the part about Dr. Ames and his affair. I am a lot of things, but I'm not a big mouth when it comes to other people's issues. Mostly because I have enough of my own issues so I don't spread news that's not mine. Katelyn sits there with her mouth open wide like she's in total shock.

"I didn't even know. Gerri came and told me I had too many hours so to leave early. I thought that was weird. You know I probably would have been in big trouble if I would have been working when this all went down."

"Let's just say that the hospital thinks I was sleep-walking."

"Vada, I don't know how you got so lucky, but I must say you are one crazy chick. Oh God...I didn't mean crazy like crazy-crazy. I meant it like crazy-funny...um..sorry."

"Oh shut up. Do you really think I am offended? I have stitches in my ass cheek, my husband just came for a booty-call, and I am an inpatient in a mental hospital. You're not even *kind of* hurting my feelings. So don't worry about it."

"Not to change the subject, but I got all my stuff from your brother

153

last night, so leaving early had its benefits."

"Oh really? That was quick. That's great!"

"Yeah, he brought the truck back and unloaded it. You wouldn't believe all the stuff I got. Some of it I need to sell, but some of it I'm going to keep because I think I've earned it. Heath helped me set everything up. Oh, and then he spent the night."

"Oh really? That was quick. That's great!" I say again, slightly mockingly.

"Are you serious or are you kidding? You're not upset or anything, are you? I think I like him." Sweet, perfect Katelyn looks at me with puppy dog eyes. I can tell she really wants my approval.

"Hell, I hope you like him if you let him spend the night the first time you hung out with the guy for crying out loud. I didn't know you were a whore Katelyn," I say laughing.

She laughs too. "I'm not a whore, but he was so nice and we got all flirty with each other. After he hooked up my TV for me, I asked him to stay for a beer. We ended up talking all night and we are going to see each other again. We have a date next weekend!"

"I'm happy for you both. Just be prepared. He sleeps with almost every female customer of his. If you pay forty dollars extra, you get the full service move."

"Shut up!"

"I'm just kidding! He's actually pretty lame. He hasn't dated anyone in a long time, so I'm glad you guys are hitting it off."

"Good. I'm glad you are okay with it. Now take your meds and ring me if you need anything. I'm here for another hour. But go to sleep; you look like you've been mauled by a tiger."

"Thank you for your kind words, ya hoe!"

"Goodnight, Vada."

"Goodnight, you brother-fucker."

"Shut up! Good night."

She is totally smitten. I haven't seen her so excited and jumpy since I met her. Her whole demeanor is different. Good for her. She shuts the big creaky door and I can hear her footsteps fade down the hallway. I must admit that I am totally shocked that perfect flawless Katelyn would be messing with my pot-head brother, but maybe they'll be good for each other. Maybe she'll give him a reason to straighten himself up. I turn off the lights and cozy up under my covers, careful to not rub any of my stitches. I can't think anymore because my medicine kicks in and I am being pulled off to a fuzzy, itchy sleep. I let go and surrender to the sandman who brings me a dream.

March 9th

I wake up to a hefty gal with a breakfast tray. I have never seen her before. She introduces herself as Sheila. She is as chipper as a freshly fucked fox. Her tight brown curls are bouncing as she walks, and she's got tie-dyed scrubs on, which are annoyingly cute. She asks me if I need anything. I just ask for my schedule and tell her I plan on leaving today.

"Oh," she says, "that's too bad. I'm new here, today's my first day. So if you are leaving this may be a short friendship!" she says chuckling at herself.

"Yep," I say. "I don't suppose you have my medicine?" I am still hurting.

"Oh my goodness gracious!" She smiles revealing plum-colored lipstick on her top front teeth. "Why here you go, lamb, I bet you are super-duper sore!"

Did she really just say that? I wonder if she'd like a super-duper black eye.

"I mean it always hurts a little worse the next day in these type of situations, but don't worry, Vada, we are going to take good care of you."

"Thank you," I say, "but like I said, I am going to be leaving here today."

She looks at me smiles and cocks her head to the side. "Yes, of course sweetie. Of course you are."

Bitch better get the hell out of my room. I don't know why this chick is rubbing me the wrong way, but I think she's being condescending and I am in no mood for this crap. My Sam Kinison internal dialogue is screaming in her face right now. Sounding a little like, "get the fuck out the dooooor! Wipe that shitty smile off your faaaaaccccce!" But I just smile, take my meds, and look at my schedule.

One on One with Rita, ten o'clock.

Evaluation, eleven thirty.

Hallelujah! I'm getting evaluated and getting the hell out of here. It was fun while it lasted but I'm ready to go get my babies! I refuse Sheila's assistance with taking a shower. I hobble my naked butt in and let the hot water run all over me. She insists on waiting outside the door in case I need anything. For goodness sake it was bruises and cuts, not head trauma. I guess this is what I get for being the dumbass that climbs a fence with barbed wire. But my shower feels delightful after the initial stinging of the sore spots. I decide to take my sweet time and sing just to annoy Sheila. I choose "Crazy Train," just to frighten her a little. I do not normally enjoy making people uncomfortable, in fact, I'm normally really freaking nice. But this whole thing has turned out to be so much work. Being here I have felt just as stressed out as I did at home. Everybody needs something. I've been taking care of my own nurse for God's sake! I'm done being nice for right now.

I get out of the shower and grab a towel and realize my clothes are out in the room. Unfortunately, so is little Miss Purple Teeth with her curly tendrils bouncing about. I cover myself as best I can and open the bathroom door. Guess who's looking at me? Yep, she's looking right at me. I try to pretend I don't notice, and start routing through my bag to find some clothes. I also need to get some under-britches and a bra. I choose some black yoga pants and a yellow flowy tank top, very casual, yet very sane. Now I must get these clothes on. I wish she would turn around. I keep my towel around my body and do the whole "junior high locker room" thing where I put my underwear on while still wrapped up. Then I must do the bra. I try to swing it into place, but my hand is still so sore I can't grab the back strap and fasten it while holding this towel. She is still watching. I am getting fussy. This must be a hoot to watch. Why the hell won't she just look away? I hate awkward situations and I'm starting to feel my inner bitch come out. Oh fuck it. I drop my towel and stand there with nothing on but pink underwear.

I throw my hands up against the pain. "Do you see them? Get a good look there, girlfriend. They are implants Sheila, but I bet you can tell that. Are you satisfied? You were betting they were fake, weren't you? Weren't you? Yep, I'm just a superficial, selfish, plastic lady who has gone mad. That's what you are thinking, right?"

She looks at me like I poked her in the eye. "I was actually looking at the drawings behind you. Perhaps you should quit being so full of yourself."

I turn around and see what she is talking about. It's the one I hung by my bed that Max made for me. It's the butt cracks picture that I hung up. Oh I am such an idiot and I feel so stupid.

"But now that you mention it, yes, I recognize that your boobs are fake. I'm so happy for you." Her voice is still an octave higher than I am comfortable with.

What do I say now? I am really looking like a crazy person. I swallow my pride and ask her to help me fasten my bra because of my stupid hand. Then I continue getting dressed. I turn and look at her and try to hold back a mixture of tears and laughter.

"That, for your information, Sheila, is a drawing of butt cracks."

She looks at me like I am the looniest toon in town, smiles a fake smile, and backs out the door.

"Ring me if you need anything, Mrs. Bower."

I realize that I have just initiated this chick on her first day as a nut-nurse. At least she'll have a good story to tell her Facebook friends.

Rita

It nears ten o'clock. I get ready to go meet up with Rita in a counseling room. I pull my hair back and dab on some lip gloss. Even though I am sore, especially my leg and butt, I push through with just a little limp. It's not that bad, but I still probably look like an idiot hobbling around. I wish I had a cane. Not because I need one, but because I've always wanted to carry a cane. I would lean on it and twirl it and maybe decorate it up a bit. I'd feel like Master Yoda walking through the halls. But no one at Rivergate Memorial Hospital or this hell hole has offered me a cane. They are probably afraid I'll beat someone with it. They are probably right.

I round the corner and see Jeremiah. He looks at me and shakes his head, but doesn't say a word. Then, he takes off in the other direction. Gee,

I wonder if he was trying to avoid me. That idiot couldn't have made it more obvious. Oh well, I'm done with him. I just need to go down about twenty more feet and I should be there. I finally make it and I see Rita sitting at an empty table. Her face lights up when I stagger in.

"Vada dear, how are you?"

"I'm great, Rita, really. I'm just inching along here."

"I heard about your accident. I was so worried. These injuries can happen in the strangest ways. I heard a story about sleepwalking. Oh dear!" she says with a tight little grin.

"Yes, I always thought it was the sheep that were supposed to jump the fence, not the people who are counting them," I say, trying to be funny, but I realize that it was a lame joke.

Rita chuckles and then her face turns more serious. She is wearing a blazer and one of the lapels is crooked and I really want to fix it. I would want someone to fix it for me. Should I do it?

"Tell me. Have you been keeping track of your meals? What are you weighing in at dear?" she asks.

I haven't kept track of anything and I have not been weighing myself. They just assume you do that here if you have an eating disorder. We are supposed to journal it. But to be honest my weight is just not on my mind right now. In fact, I have probably lost weight in the last week being here because I haven't been snacking and I've been on so many meds. My pants are feeling a bit looser.

"Yes Rita, I have. I am doing great. I feel great, aside from all the stitches and welts and bruises. I feel like a million bucks. I haven't been doing any purging and I haven't even thought about it."

"Well, darling, I would love to believe that is true. I see so much potential in you Vada. You know though dear-heart, we recently found vomit on your clothing."

Oh freaking bloody hell. I was on opiates! Pain medication! Who doesn't puke on pain medicine?

"Well, Rita," I say, "my medicine made me sick. Wait a minute, how on earth did you find that out?

"I don't think that is important."

"Just tell me...How do you know there was puke on my clothes?"

"Well, if you must know, one of the staff members found a sweatshirt with vomit on it in your room and felt it was something I needed to know about. I believe this person was correct. All of our staff looks out for our patients."

That dirty, sneaky, redneck asshole Jeremiah! What the hell is his problem? He may be mad about me not coming out when he was there to pick me up, but he didn't have to go and do something like that. What a turd. He must have just found it right after I left my room and ran this info to Rita. Unless...he was in my room while I was sleeping! Eww...that creeps me out!

"Rita, I can promise you that I was not making myself throw up. I don't tolerate pain meds well. As for Jeremiah, he can stay away from me. I have a feeling he was in my room last night, and that is a violation...a security...."

"Who is Jeremiah? Vada, you are not making sense. I don't know anyone with that name." Her face is truly concerned.

"Oh, he's the janitor. I'm sorry, I just thought..."

"Vada, I don't know who this is or why you are fraternizing with the

160

janitorial staff, but let's be clear. The person who shared this information was looking out for your best interests."

"Oh freaking spare me this crap Rita! Let's knock off the bullshit and tell me who it was."

"Fine, it was Sheila, the new day nurse we have added to our staff. "

"That bitch!" I am almost yelling and realize I need to calm down.

"Oh my, Vada. You are so angry, dear. We need to address this."

"No! No! I am not angry. See? I am happy. I'm just defending myself from false accusations."

"Vada, at this time I would like you to do some breathing exercises. Just calm down...in and out...in and out."

I'm sorry. But my mother is not paying an arm and a leg for this bitch to tell me how to breathe. For heaven sake it's already cost her two toes. In fact, I believe people start practicing breathing in utero, so this is some really messed up shit. I don't know why I am so angry, but these people are so bass-akwards. Instead of providing a calming and healthy environment, they are just continually pissing me off. I need a Xanax. But I breathe like an idiot and do my best to swallow my craziness.

Rita looks at me with a smile and says, "I feel like you are letting anger get in the way of your treatment. Let's try the breathing when you start to feel rage. Now Vada, I am going to have to ask you to step on the scale. We are focused on health, not numbers, but you have not been tracking this information and I know that because I have seen no documentation of this since you were first admitted. Let's just hop up on the square in the corner over here, alright?"

"Sure," I say. I walk over to the white floor scale. The digital numbers pop up and to my surprise there they are—105. Oh holy hell. For the first time in my life I am not happy that I have lost weight.

"Vada, clearly you can understand my concern."

"Rita, look, I totally get it, okay? But you have to understand I was getting ready to start my period when I came here. I always gain water weight around that time. I'm done now and I'm sure that explains it, plus the medicine I've been on hasn't made me quite as hungry. Please believe me when I tell you this. I am not throwing up! Not on purpose!"

"Darling..."

"Don't 'darling' me Rita, I am fine. I haven't puked since that night in the bathroom, (which never happened anyways) so get over it and get my husband here to pick me up now!"

Rita throws her hands up and shakes her head. She starts writing on a clipboard and I almost lose it. Breathe, Vadie, fucking breathe. Maybe this bitch was on to something with the breathing after all.

"Vada, I want you to know where we stand. I am giving you an *opportunity* to tell me the truth right here and now. Do you realize what I am saying to you? Here is your *opportunity*."

She says the word *opportunity* like it's a word from a 40's musical number.

"Well Rita, thank you for the *opportunity,* but since you don't believe anything that I say, I am evoking my Fifth Amendment right. I can't quite remember exactly what that means. However, I do know that it has something to do with the fact that I don't have to talk to you anymore. So shoo fly! Don't bother me! Go find some other troubled girl to save."

"I think we are done for now, Vada. You may return to your room. We will see you for your evaluation at eleven thirty. Just remember, I was trying to give you a chance."

I get up and walk out. No, I don't walk out. I hobble out like Igor. What is Rita talking about anyways? I'm so confused, but too pissed to think about it. I'm mad and grumpy and have an expression on my face that probably looks like I just ate a bag of shit. As I make my way down the hall, I see her coming at me. I think she's going to charge me like a bull. She has those crazy eyes and her stringy hair is in her face. Her gray matching sweat suit has pit stains, and looks like a 70's high school gym uniform. I close my eyes and brace myself as Bath Salts Mary comes leaping and pummels me like a linebacker. I fall to the ground and my head hits the marble floor. Oh my God ouch. The pain in my head makes my eyes hurt and I am totally disoriented. Water fills my eyes. The cut on my back feels like it's been torn open, but I don't feel any blood coming out. What the hell is wrong with this person? I think she may have just tried to kill me. I'm going to play dead. If I move I could possibly get it again. I'm just going to lay here and hope someone comes to help before my face gets eaten. I bet she's going to eat my eyes out first. So I keep them shut tight. Bath Salts Mary says nothing, but I can hear several people pulling her off of me. I know one voice is Rita, the other one Jeremiah. They have taken her off into a room and hopefully shot her crazy ass with a syringe full of chill-the-fuck-out. I open my eyes and to my surprise I see my sandwich friend; the pretty one from the group meeting, standing over me. I also see several nurses and some stunned patients staring as if they've never seen a girl get tackled before. The next thing I know I am in an office lying on what seems to be a hospital bed, one with the side rails and a tray.

I'm shocked to discover that my sandwich friend is holding an ice pack on my head.

"Hey you," she says.

"What just happened?"

"It appears you may have an enemy. You were attacked by another patient and you have a pretty bad bump on your head. You are going to be fine. You don't have any signs of a concussion, just a nasty bump."

"Well, isn't that just dandy," I say. "You look familiar. I thought you were a patient."

"Oh no. Although sometimes I feel like I could be. I've got four kids at home and I swear sometimes I'm going to lose my mind."

"Oh. I know how that feels. Do you mind telling me what the hell that crazy bitch's problem is?"

"Oh Vada, I think she's protecting her territory. You see, I am a nurse practitioner. I am here for medical treatment, not mental health purposes. Most of the patients don't know that and I tend to get an earful of gossip whether I want to hear it or not."

"What are you saying? Are you saying there are rumors going around?"

"Not necessarily, but I do know that Mary Weaverton has a crush on the janitor and I think she may have an inkling that he likes you."

"That's ridiculous! I am married and I wouldn't touch him with a ten foot pole! Eww...not only is it him, but do you know where that thing has been? And who it has been in? Yuck." Mary must know that he gave me a ride to the country club the other night.

"Oh I know that, and you know that. But that lady for some reason does not know that."

"Lady, my ass! I bet her mother was an elephant and her father was the Hunchback of Notre Dame. She is not a lady. She's a garbage truck with legs! You seem like a normal person. I think everyone else here is nuttier than a bunch of fruitcakes. Can you please try and tell them to let me out of here?"

"I'm going to get your evaluation team. They are the ones you should be speaking with about this. I am just here to fix the boo-boos."

She leaves the room and I sit and wait. This whole thing is absurd. Several minutes pass and she comes back in with her pretty face and tells me that I am free to head to Dr. Lipton's office. I feel like I should be wearing a damn helmet and possibly a bullet proof vest at this point but my sandwich friend assures me that they've got "Miss Weaverton" in isolation. Walking down the hall, a sense of total anxiety washes over me like a torrential downpour. I am sweaty and tense and want to jump out of my skin. I know I am about to face the panel. It's like the first day of high school. I can't even think I am so nervous. I take my stupid deep breaths and try to fake the fear that I can feel from my head to my ass and down to my toes. I turn the corner into the big room that is set up like a dinner party. Dr. Lipton, Dr. Ames, Rita, and Amelia Peters, hospital administrator, are all seated and waiting for me, the late guest, to arrive. Everyone has a drink in front of them, coffee or water, and they all look as cozy and comfortable as if they were getting ready for their appetizers to arrive. I stumble in and take a seat in an empty chair. They are all looking very serious. Ms. Peters has on a red silk button down shirt and a charcoal pencil skirt. Her red lipstick is glistening in the recessed lighting.

"Well Mrs. Bower, how are you today?" asks Ms. Peters.

"I am just lovely," I say, even though I'm covered in stitches and just got my ass kicked by a woman twice my size.

"We are all here, as you know, to evaluate both your progress thus far, and to determine your needs for future care. We understand that this may have been a difficult week here at New Outlook for you, and we want you to know that your well-being is our number one concern."

"Thanks." I'm trying to control my anxiety, but I feel like a spider has been turned loose in my underwear and I want to run out screaming. "So what is the verdict?"

Dr. Lipton immediately chimes in, "Vada, I feel that there has been some progress made in the last week. You have shared with me many of your experiences and I think you have been able to identify triggers and hopefully have learned how to cope when things begin to weigh you down. I see some positives."

"Well, that's just wonderful." Okay, maybe this isn't going to be so bad after all.

"I would also like to stress to you the importance of taking care of yourself and as we have discussed, making time for yourself."

"Yes, I know I need to do that. I'm going to start bowling or something." This is total bullshit because I hate bowling and I would never wear rented shoes. Can you imagine the amount of fecal matter inside of the bowling ball holes? Bowling alleys are disgusting!

Dr. Lipton looks over at Rita. She seems to want to take it from here and I fear this could be a shit show.

"Okay, from my personal experience with you Vada, I still see a lot of denial. You have lost weight since you have been here. I've on several occasions found evidence of purging. I feel that you are still at a high-risk level and that you have a way to go. On a positive note, I do think that you have made many personal relationships during your stay which tells me you have probably found ways to relate to others in recovery. That is crucial."

"May I just say one thing?" I ask. "I am not trying to interrupt but I am not really bulimic. I have tried to tell you that. I made it up okay? It was all BS. I tried to puke one time at my house. It didn't even work. I've only lost weight because I have been on so much medication..."

They are all staring at me. Their eyes are glued to my face. It almost hurts. I wish they would stop staring at me. Oh yes, and then they do. Just long enough to exchange worrisome glances and jot down some notes.

"We know that, Vada." says Dr. Lipton. He glances at Dr. Ames and nods.

"You do?" I ask.

Dr. Ames pulls out a tape recorder. What is that for? What the hell is he going to do with it? He pops in a tape and places his hand over it almost like he is afraid I'm going to snatch it and throw it against the wall. He's probably smart to think so.

"Given your diagnosis Vada..." says Dr. Lipton.

"And what is that exactly?" I ask. "No one has ever even mentioned to me what the hell I am diagnosed with! So you tell me Dr. Lipton, what is it that Vada Bower has, huh? I know it's not an eating disorder. Do you know how I know that? Because I love fried chicken. I love pizza and chocolate and beer. I love corndogs and milkshakes. I also love digesting these things and then having a nice relaxing crap. So go on, spill it. I think I should know my diagnosis, don't you?"

"As I told you, we know you aren't bulimic Vada. That's why your diagnosis is complicated."

"Uh..umm," Dr. Ames clears his throat. "I think that it is time you took a listen to your hypnosis sessions, Vada. I thought you would have recalled this information by now, but seeing as though you haven't, I do think from a doctor to a patient, that it is important for you to know."

This is kind of scaring me. What could I have said during hypnosis?

"Okay, that is fine. Let's hear it."

Everyone knows something. I feel like there is an elephant in the room and I am the only one who cannot see it.

"I assume that you have all already had the pleasure of listening to

167

my tapes, am I right?" I ask.

They nod. What a bunch of freaking donkeys.

"Alright then, Vada, we'll start with this recording from your first hypnosis." Dr. Ames clicks a button with a blue arrow. All I can think is that tape recorder looks like it's from the early 90's and I am anticipating hearing some funky beats once it starts rolling. It doesn't. No music plays. I hear Dr. Ames' voice, sounding like he's reading a bed time story and I can barely make out what he is saying. Now I hear my voice. It's sleepy and slow, but it is definitely mine. I brace myself for what I am about to hear. It sounds like he's starting in the middle of a session.

Me: Yes.

Dr. Ames: What worries you the most Vada?

Me: That I am a bad mother.

Dr. Ames: What makes you think you are a bad mother?

Me: I am away from my kids. I am in here.

Dr. Ames: You are in here for treatment for mental health. I want you to understand that it is okay to take care of yourself, Vada. You are helping yourself so that you can help your children. Do you believe that?

Me: I don't know.

Dr. Ames: You don't know what? You don't know that you are in a mental health recovery center?

Me: I know that.

Dr. Ames: Then what don't you know, Vada?

Me: I don't know if I need to be here.

Dr. Ames: Why do you say that Vada? What makes you think that you shouldn't be here?

Me: Because...none of it...is true. I made it all up.

He stops the tape. I am sitting in front of this panel. They are all judging me and it's not for my singing voice. They all seem to know something that I don't. I have the funniest inkling after hearing that, that I recall that conversation. I kind of remember saying that now. Oh Lord!

"There is a diagnosis out there Vada. It is referred to as mythomania, or more commonly known as pathological or compulsive lying. I am not saying that we believe you are a pathological liar. I want to make sure you understand the difference between..."

I cut him off. "I'm not a pathological liar, you guys. It's not even like that. I meant that I was lying about..."

"It's my turn to interrupt," says Dr. Ames with all his chins. "There is another section of tape that I'd like for you to hear before we go on," he says in a tone that makes me want to take an ice pick to his scrotum sack and remove his teeny tiny balls. He hits the forward button and then the blue arrow. There's my sleepy voice again.

Dr. Ames: What have you accomplished so far in your stay here at New Outlook?

Me: Well, I have eaten delicious brownies. I helped Katelyn lose her low-life boyfriend. I helped Jessalyn expose her perverted pedophile grandfather. I tried so hard to help Lauren with her birthday party. I helped Bath Salt's Mary's boyfriend treat her right.

Dr. Ames: Okay Vada, now let me ask this in a different way, what have you done here at New Outlook that has benefitted *you*? Just you and your recovery?

Me: I ate delicious brownies. I got a hold of the janitor's carpet cleaner and cleaned the carpet in my room twice. I got a mop and spray cleaner and scrubbed my bathroom floors sometimes more than once a day. I really like clean floors.

Dr. Ames: Yes, Vada. The floors are important to you. All the headaches you've experienced, tell me about those.

Me: I was faking them.

Dr. Ames stopped the tape. The panel looks at me as if I would have been voted off if this were elimination night.

Dr. Lipton starts flapping his jaws. "You see, Vada. This is significant. We feel that a diagnosis of obsessive compulsive disorder needs to be made. This floor cleaning is not healthy and is a control issue for you. Do you realize that now?"

What am I supposed to say? Of course I am OCD about the floor. Why don't they just fry me in the electric chair for it? I'm guilty. It's not like it's hurting anybody. In fact, I'm helping the struggling economy by purchasing cleaning supplies.

"Yes, I do, I'm going to leave my floors dirty for a while. I'll only mop every other day. Will that work for all of you? Can we please end this now, so I can go home?"

"Just one more moment..." Rita whispers in Dr. Lipton's ear and he then whispers in Dr. Ames' ear who then whispers in Ms. Peters' ear.

"Oooh are we playing telephone, should I scoot closer?" I ask.

They all ignore my attitude and Dr. Ames puts in a new tape. We listen. This is just dreadful. I don't want to hear any more of this ridiculous pig shit.

Dr. Ames: Tell me Vada, about when you were going to commit suicide on the roof.

Me: I wasn't. I just needed to get a break…

Dr. Ames: A break, like a broken tailbone, arm, leg? Were you looking to break a bone?"

Me: I just needed a break. I didn't care where it was.

Dr. Ames: So you weren't actually trying to kill yourself?

Me: No, just a break. I tried to make it quick.

He stopped the tape. I see what these bastards are getting at. They are trying to make it look like I wanted to hurt myself.

"Just a minute, I did *not* break anything! I meant a break like I needed a motherfucking break! Like a minute to myself! Haven't you people ever had kids? Do they not make you want to run out screaming sometimes? Do your relatives not make you want to hide? Well mine FUCKING do! So I went on the roof to hide. When I said I didn't care where it was, I meant a place...not a body part! A sabbatical, not a broken bone. You are manipulating my words!" I am now shouting. I am sounding like one of the crazies. This is what I have resorted to. I'm going mad. They are not listening and I know it.

"Vada, we have discussed this as a group of trained professionals. We all agree that you have a mental illness which is considered a factitious disorder. There are different degrees and types of factitious disorders including one called Munchausen syndrome. We are not talking about by proxy, not the one where you would fake someone else's illness, like a child's. We are talking about faking your own. The constant headaches, while refusing pain relievers and you've admitted you have been faking

171

them. The neck problems you've described in your sessions that appear to come and go with no explanation. This is a complicated diagnosis. Factitious disorder can go hand in hand with other mental illness, in your case, obsessive compulsive disorder and anxiety. We believe that your incident on the roof was a way for you to injure yourself to seek medical attention. Your plan was interrupted because your husband caught you in the act. In addition, we do *not* in fact feel you have an eating disorder but you do have a very real need for people to *think* you have an eating disorder. We believe that the evidence of this has been deliberately staged by you. Please know we are not judging you. We believe we can help you."

My blood is boiling. They have this all wrong. I look at Rita. "Then what the hell were you acting so concerned for?"

She replies most definitely, "I was giving you the *opportunity* to come clean, Vada."

There she goes with that stupid word again, opportunity.

"I specialize in eating disorders and was immediately suspicious that something was off with your case that night in the bathroom. I wasn't positive so I simply did my part to support you and gave you the benefit of the doubt. I gave you the chance to tell me the truth many times."

Dr. Lipton's voice overpowers the conversation. "It has become clear that you have established several relationships with other patients and while we commend you in your efforts to try and help them, it is our collective opinion that you are seeking relationships in order to increase the people in your life who will believe in your (and he finger quotes) 'illnesses.' I do, however, believe, as you stated in one of our sessions that you have always felt forgotten, like when you were left at the grocery store as a child. I think that factitious disorder can stem from these types of feelings and incidents."

"That's just not true. First of all I was never left at the fucking grocery store!" I argue. "Secondly, I have tried to help some of these women because I am a mother! That's what I do. It's not attention-seeking or manipulative. It's a maternal instinct for shit's sake!"

Dr. Lipton won't shut up. "In addition, we have come to the conclusion that your 'sleepwalking' incident the other night was in fact a deliberate need to seek medical attention and attention from other patients. Injuring one's self is a very common part of this illness. At this time, the fact that you are seriously hurting yourself is extremely concerning and I'm afraid we cannot release you. You are at high-risk for causing further damage and harming yourself."

My eyes dart at Dr. Ames who will not look me in the eye.

"You dirty piece of shit!" I say to him. "You lied to me. You know what happened that night with the fence. Tell them about the security tape! Why don't you speak up?"

"Vada, we are going to have to ask you to calm down. Remember you came to us for help. That is all we are trying to give you," Ms. Peters says calmly.

"That's right. I did. Didn't I? I came here for help. Actually, you know what? I'm done with his whole thing. I didn't really come here for help." I stand up. "I came here to get away for a while. I just wanted a vacation alone, but couldn't justify going to the beach without my family. Your fancy brochures looked so wonderful." My hands are now waving around and I'm losing my patience. "I was thinking… nice rooms, sleeping all night without a baby crying. I was going to do yoga, which by the way is a joke. I faked this whole stupid thing so that I could have some peace and quiet! You guys have obviously not figured this out by now. Hello...McFly? Don't you get it? There is nothing wrong with me! I came here on purpose to get some time to MYSELF. I am perfectly healthy. This is such a misunderstanding. I just need to get home."

Dr. Lipton stands up. He frowns and removes his stupid looking glasses. "We know you are physically healthy Vada. That's the problem.

Your repeated attempts at creating mental and physical illness and now injuring yourself are a mental illness in itself. Planting vomit on a sweatshirt which you know would be found...I'm sorry Vada. We cannot release you. You came in voluntarily, but as your doctors we have the legal rights to keep you here for your own safety. I think its best you return to your room for the night and we will discuss this further with you tomorrow. We have an extensive treatment plan waiting for you."

"Fuck! Off!" I yell.

I move my chair out of the way and head for the door. Dr. Ames blocks my path. I see him send a message on his computer and shadows on the etched glass door tell me that he has called security.

"Are you kidding me, you jerk off? I want to get home to my children! I need to be with my babies. Fuck you! Let me out of this shitty hospital. I'll sue every one of your asses, do you hear me?" I'm yelling so loud that I'm surprising myself.

I'm getting out of here one way or another. I push Dr. Lipton out of the way and he yields, to my surprise. I open the door and find myself surrounded by three men in white scrubs. I'm five foot tall. Do they really think it's going to take this many grown men to get me? Idiots!

"We can do this the easy way or the hard way Vada. Just let them walk you to your room." I know its Dr. Ames' voice.

"He's fucking the nurse! The one with the plastic face!" I yell, pointing at Dr. Ames. "You are a cheating pig! I'm going to tell your wife! What about my box, huh? You just completely fucked my box!"

What does it matter? They all just think I'm spouting off crazy talk and they probably think I'm talking about my vagina. I feel so helpless. What have I done? I really did just want a quick week away from home. Just some rest. I wanted to come right back home and be the best mom in the world like I always am. This whole thing has gone way too far. But I'm not going to my room. I'm getting out of here, because I'm not a prisoner. I have three children who have had their mom gone long enough. I'm so out of here. I immediately look for the best possible route. The hall to the left leads to patient rooms. The hall to my right leads to the Solarium and I could run out the back door in to the wooded trails. Alright. Here goes nothing. I bolt. Who knew it would come to this? The guards are right on my trail and I pass patients gawking at me in my high speed chase. I'm running as if my life depends on it. I see Katelyn as I make the turn into the Solarium.

"Vada!" she yells stunned. I just keep going. I'm still so sore from my stitches that I know I'm not running at my full potential, but my adrenaline is through the roof and I push through the pain. I do think I have popped a stitch or two in my leg though. All I can hear is my heart beat and all I can think of is getting out the door. If I can make it to the trails, I can hide. I know I can do this.

I see the door to the outside and it's daytime, so it should be unlocked. I don't even slow down. I slam into the door and push the bar to open it. This literally backfires because they've put the place on lockdown. I fall back and slam my head on the marble floor. Fuck that hurt. How many times does a girl have to land on her head! I turn over to get up when I am surrounded. I have two men restraining each arm and one holding my legs. My horrific vision has come true. I am being held down against my will looking like the Exorcist and shouting profanities. "Get off me, you cocksuckers!" I yell. I am thrashing and shouting, but I still have control of my bladder. "Get your hands off me, assholes!" This is all seems impossible. Like it's a dream...I feel like biting these pricks, but the next thing I know, I feel a sharp stick in my thigh, there goes the bladder, and I am spinning into a world of darkness.

Waking up is hard to do

"Vada? Are you awake?"

175

No. I am not. I am not. I'm sunk down and I can't open my eyes. I'm not on a normal level of consciousness, but I hear a voice.

"Vada? Are you ready to wake up?"

Who is this talking to me? Where am I? Where are my boys? Where is Eric? Where is this voice coming from? Am I dead? I try hard to force my eyes to open and all I can see is gray walls. There are only gray stone walls and no windows. I fall back asleep.

"Vada Bower...I need to you to try and sit up."

That voice. Who is it? My eyes open and I am relieved. What a nightmare! This is the worst dream I have ever had. I sit up and realize that I am not in my normal bed. I am in a hospital bed. There are restraints hanging loosely on each side of me. Shit this is real, this was not a dream. I am in isolation. It's all coming back to me.

Two months later

I am sitting in the front row of Max and Ben's end of the year school program with Jordan on my lap. This is the first big school event that I've been to since I got out of the nuthouse. I have on a yellow spring dress and my hair is down and freshly highlighted. Although, they'd never know by looking at me, I can't help but feel slightly paranoid that some of the other parents may have suspicions. The mother who is involved in every activity, every sport, every party, doesn't just disappear for three and a half weeks. That's how long I was there. The longest three and a half weeks of my life. It probably would have been more if I hadn't finally convinced Amelia Peters, with Katelyn's help, that Dr. Ames was trying to make me look crazy, so no one would believe me if I told anyone about his affair. So what? Maybe I faked, or "embellished" a little bit to get into a luxury psyche ward, but that was on purpose. Many of the other patients and even little lunch lady, Loretta went to bat for me. Jessalyn talked to Rita, who is still her sponsor, and told her the real story with my sneak out and the fence incident. I was assigned new therapists and Dr. Ames has been put on paid leave while an investigation is being done. The fact that he destroyed the tapes from that night, seemed to work as evidence on my side. Katelyn says he is still not back at work. Good, because Mrs. Ames got a very revealing letter about her husband…from me. I hope she kicks his ass out. That idiot!

I have stayed in touch with Jessalyn. A couple weeks after leaving the looney bin, she took everything she owned and decided to find a new life for herself out in New York City. She's already booked a few modeling jobs and I know she's going to do great. I'm excited for her. This suburban paradise is no place for a model. She literally left her past behind her. Plus, I think Sabrina and I are going to try and plan a weekend to go and see her in the fall. I just hope there aren't many biker bars in NYC! But if there are, we know how to close them down.

Lauren Sanders got out of there too. Unfortunately, it was not to a better place. She's been transferred to a more intensive treatment center in Missouri. I do keep in touch with her though and have sent her a birthday card every day since I have been out. The poor thing has no family, but I'm at least thankful we gave her at least one happy day. I hope the cards help. I occasionally get a letter back addressed to "SHITHEAD" and it's always the same story about the day she was born. At least writing letters gives her something to do. I guess sometimes I wish I had the balls to call people shitheads out loud. I kind of admire the lady.

As far as I'm concerned, Bath Salts Mary should be locked up forever and sterilized. I don't know what the hell that swollen beastly woman is up to these days, but I am constantly worried that I will wake up one night and she'll be peeking up at me with those ghastly eyes from the foot of my bed just licking her chops. I haven't seen her since the attack in the hallway, but I hope she and her venereal diseases live happily ever after, and far, far away from me!

If anything else good came out of this whole thing, it is that I now cherish every waking moment of time I have with my children. I know I will have moments. I know that things will get stressful. However, I know

now that any amount of time with them is important for them and for me.

I look over and see Heath and Katelyn (holding hands) to my left, Eric to my right and my three-toed mother and goofy father next to him, all there to watch my boys sing some songs and be as cute as can be. Sabrina is right behind me along with Eric's parents. I feel so lucky to have all of these people here who love me and most importantly, love my kids. Jordan is already starting to squirm, but I don't care. He's a baby and that's what babies do.

I've decided that when all the other moms ask me where I have been, I will simply say "I had to have my spleen removed after a series of tests." I've practiced the line many times. It rolls right off the tongue. I'm not really sure what a spleen is, but I Googled it and I know it can be removed and you can live without it. It's in your guts somewhere, so clearly no one will miss it. What the hell...I know it's not that exciting, but it's simple and I don't owe anyone any explanations. I'm allowed to have some privacy.

I watch my boys sing their songs. Between each song all the parents clap and Sabrina is doing the whole "woop-woop" thing and you can hear her over everyone else. My boys know it's her and are eating it up. I know that my ridiculous eyes are full of tears, but I can't help but feel so overwhelmed that I get to be their mom. They are wonderful. Max has one finger up his nose. Ben seems to keep checking to make sure his wiener is still there. They are my perfect boys and I have the most amazing crazy life I could ever imagine.

Since I have been home, I told Eric the truth. I spilled the beans about everything, from start to finish. Although, I got a lecture on being honest with him from now on, I think he actually understood. I remember him saying, "It shouldn't have had to take something so drastic for me to realize that you need a break once in a while." With that comment, I knew we would be okay. He still pisses me off quite easily, but he's stood by me and I appreciate that. Sometimes, he even cleans up his own spills...well...sometimes.

For the record, I'm still on medication. But you know what? Looking around at the crowd of mothers sitting here tonight, I bet at least half of us are. The other half are thinking about making an appointment to get some. I'd bet my left implant on it.

Doing the Mom Thing

Thank you followers for not abandoning me. I know it's been a while since I have posted, but please know that I'm back and I'm more excited about being real than ever before. I will keep this short today, because I've promised my kiddos I'd build them a fort to sleep in tonight. That should be fun...especially once it's done and they *still* want to sleep in my bed. Lol! But I wanted to at least give my fellow mothers some thoughts for today.

1. Whatever happens during your day, always know you *could* have a raging yeast infection that would make it a lot worse. And if you're unfortunate enough to currently have a yeast infection, I would recommend you get that cleared up as soon as possible. Just sayin'.

2. Don't feel like you're crazy or alone because it gets hard sometimes. If you feel like crying just fucking do it. Don't hold it in. Some mothers go a little nutty because they worry too much. Some lose it because they forget to take care of themselves. Some mothers are depressed as hell. Some mothers may just feel overwhelmed. You may be obsessive-compulsive, or you may be constantly paranoid that you are just not good enough. Then again, there are some who are just bitches...and there's no treatment for that. We all have a little bit of crazy in us, and that is okay. We are martyrs. We are warriors. We are mothers. We are the ones God chose for our children. Be who you are, because that is who your children need you to be. Unless you do bath salts...and in that case I would contact your local law enforcement agency and have your children taken to a safe place because that is just not okay.

3. Take one night a week and do something for yourself. Whether it's a

movie, a trip to the store alone, or dinner with a friend, just do it. If you possibly can, take a weekend trip once a year with a friend or your husband. Get your "me time." If you don't, you could end up in a looney bin somewhere...and wouldn't Vegas or Jamaica be so much better? I'm vowing to do this from now on, and I suggest you do too. I will not feel guilty. I am still going to be the best fucking mommy in the world and so will you. No guilt. Let your conscience be as clean as the floor you walk on (and if it's not then grab a broom and a mop) and give yourself a break once in a while. You know you need it.

I appreciate you sticking with me. Find out what happens over the next few months when I have to find ways to entertain my three boys all summer long. This could get interesting. I know it will be fine, though. I have a new outlook on life. I'm going to stay strong and do what I do. But on the inside, I'm still going to say fuck a lot.

Thanks for reading!

~Vada Nicole Bower...and proud of it!

The End

ACKNOWLEDGEMENTS

So many amazing people in my life have believed in me enough that I dared to write a book way outside of my comfort zone. My children and husband who are the reason I get up in the morning, literally, like early...every morning are my motivation for everything I do.

I have to thank my mother who always said, "who cares what people say...fuck 'em if they can't take a joke." I love you mom. Thank you to my dad and my brother Paul, who make my life amazingly wonderful and complicated. Paul, I will always be your biggest fan. Thank you for being a tough critic, you bastard. Dad, you're an idiot and I love you dearly.

Thank you to Amber Yoshida for designing and shooting my cover photo. All of your work is amazing and I want to be like you!

My friends! Jenn, who shares my sick sense of humor. Cristy, who gets all the craziness in my life. Thanks to Katie, Audrey, Allison, Annie, Lori, Stephanie, and all of the ladies that have gone out of their way to show support. All my friends whose little guys are buddies of my little guys...you are all awesome!

Many thanks to all of my cousins and aunts and uncles in Kansas, Illinois, Nebraska, and Missouri...all of you have been so supportive in helping me spread the word and believing in me. Thank you Sara for signing my credit card slip that day...Thanks to my sweet and precious grandparents, who said, "It's okay Krissy, we've heard bad words before."

All of my friends and family! Thanks a million!

I would also like to add here, that all of the characters in this book are purely fictional. Any resemblances to persons living or dead are purely coincidental. The names of towns and places, other than Kansas City are also fictional. The New Outlook Center for Mental and Behavioral Health in this book is a fictional place in the fictional town of Rivergate. In other words, this is all pure fiction.

The Vada Diaries

Short Stories and Confessions of a Crazy Mother

By Kristen Lynn

Vada Bower, stay-at-home mother of three, has a crazy life, like most mothers. These are some of her thoughts and experiences *before* her stay in the mental institution. This is meant to be a companion piece to the full-length novel, *The Unbalancing Act.*

Contents

"Dedicated to…..LMC"

A Day at the Park

That stupid sonofabitch almost got his ass knocked the fuck out. Who in the hell does he think he is anyway? He messed with the wrong person today. That's for sure.

I got up off the brown metal park bench and confronted my enemy. He held his fists firmly by his hips like he was about to start some shit. I couldn't help but notice that he must have had a peanut butter and jelly sandwich for lunch, as jelly marks smiled up the corners of his mouth. I was just dying to pull out a wet wipe at that very moment and clean his stupid face, but I knew I needed to set aside my compulsions and take care of business. I lifted my white-framed sunglasses off my face and set them on the top of my head, holding back my brown hair, which I actually took the time to curl today. Thank you very much. This dude was not going to screw up the one day all week that I had looked in the mirror.

I crossed my arms and made the meanest face I could. At that point, it was on like Donkey Kong. It was a stand-off, each of us not knowing who would speak first. He was such a little troll. His pockets hung out of his jeans and his stained white T-shirt was less than intimidating. He almost looked scared for a minute, once he realized I wasn't backing down. What a turd. I thought to myself, *here's your chance Vada. Nail this prick.*

"Hey you," I finally said. My voice sounded way too *momish*, so I tried it again. "Hey, I'm talking to you!" I said in a much meaner voice.

"What?" replied the little shit.

"Are you picking on my kid?"

That little asshole was at least nine years old, and a little on the beefy side. I would bet he eats off the extra-value menu. He was definitely too damn big to be picking on a six year old, especially my six year old. I am medicated for a reason, and my mama bear instinct means that bad things can happen if my kids get messed with.

"Who are you?" asked Little Bully. I bet this turd looks like his dad. I bet his dad is a douche.

"I'm your worst nightmare," I said. "You like picking on little kids? Do ya? Does it make you feel like a big tough guy? My kid is so much freaking cooler than you. You probably don't even wipe."

"I'm gonna tell my mom!" he says.

"Oh, you want your mommy? Do ya? Poor little bully. What would your mommy think if she knew you pushed Benjamin down and told him he couldn't play kickball with you guys? He can play kickball anytime he wants to. It's not his fault that you don't want to lose to a smaller kid. Now let's play some ball. Oh wait," I said, with one hand holding the ball in the air, the other hand on my chin, "You can't play, because you're a bully. Go home."

He looked at me like he was going to cry and I noticed that an audience of children was starting to form. I knew that if they started chanting, "fight, fight, fight" I couldn't lose to that donkey. I knew I had to end this quickly. "Anyway, it's *our* ball," I said. "We brought it from *our* house, and you can't play with *my* son because you are not nice!"

I looked at Ben with a big smile and said, "Hey little buddy, you pitch!" I looked around at the non-bullying children and hollered, "Kids, get in your places." Yep, that's me, the biggest badass mama on the planet, at least once in a while.

The kids all scattered, each running to their positions, except for Little Bully. He ran off toward the houses that border the field.

I took a seat on the sidelines with Jordan, who I let out of the stroller to run around. My five year old, Max, hadn't witnessed this incident and was playing on the playground behind me. It was the perfect fall day. I knew there wouldn't be many more before that mother cunt named "winter" set in, bringing seasonal depression with her, so I was glad we were out enjoying the sunshine. Apparently, I wasn't the only one who felt this way because the park was freaking packed. I was thankful that most of the moms were too busy chatting with each other to notice that I just kicked a child out of a public park.

The teams switched over and Ben was up to kick. I love my boys so much. They are so amazing. The thought of anyone ever picking on them makes my blood just boil. It's not their fault they are so cute. They also happen to be small for their age. I'm only five foot tall and my husband, Eric, isn't so tall himself. Our boys just don't have much hope in the height department. I'm probably too protective, but hey, I'm protective of all kids, and I would absolutely let my kids have it if they ever picked on anyone. I certainly wouldn't stand for them treating someone the way Little Bully treated Ben.

Ben kicked the ball and it went flying. Fuck yes, that's my baby!

"Go Benny man! Go!" I yelled. That's right. He totally showed those bitches what's up. He made it to third. See, it was worth it. Baby Jordan was even clapping for him. Oh, brotherly love! I am the luckiest mom in the world. I honestly didn't think anything could ruin this day for me. My crazy pills were definitely working. The only thing that would have made it better is if Eric would have been there, but he was gone all week on business.

While enjoying my kids, I watched a yellow butterfly flutter around in front of us and it caught Jordan's eye too. He got up and chased it. I took my camera phone out from my over-packed bag and snapped some shots. This was the cutest thing I had ever seen. I couldn't have felt more complete at that moment. I swear, I almost heard background music in my mind, that's how picture perfect this moment was.

Then, I felt two sweet arms around my neck. It was my Max. "Hey sweet boy, you having fun?" I asked.

"Yep," he said. "Mommy? Did you kick a kid?"

I looked at him perplexed, "No honey, why would you ask me that?"

"That boy over there told me you kicked his brother."

"Oh Lord, he has a brother?" I asked. I see who he's talking about, and it's a smaller and younger version of that little dipshit, like one isn't enough already.

"He said his brother went home to tell his mommy that you kicked him."

"I didn't kick him Max. I kicked him out of the game because he was being unkind. He pushed Ben down and teased him, and that's just not acceptable."

Max just stared at me with his blue-green eyes, off in thought somewhere. Jordan was still running around after the butterfly.

"Go play sweetie, don't worry about it. If his mommy comes I will tell her that her son was not being nice, and that he needs to practice making better choices and treating other kids the way he would like to be treated." I kissed his soft little face.

As Max ran back to the playground, I checked my phone to see what time it was. It was about four o'clock. I made a mental note that we had better leave in about ten minutes. Eric was coming home soon and I thought I should probably make dinner. I hate making dinner. Then I thought, screw it. I'm ordering pizza. Who do people think I am anyway, The Pioneer Woman? Not hardly. I can fuck up macaroni and cheese, and have many times. Yeah, pizza would do just fine.

I grabbed little Jordan, whose butterfly friend had flown away, and I tickled his tummy. We were practically making out when I heard a child's voice yelling from off in the distance. "There she is! It's that short lady that looks like a kid!"

I looked up to see what I can only describe as a female wrestler, with a tight red perm about two inches long all the way around her giant head. It was like Little Orphan Annie on steroids. Good Lord. She was running with all her might. The amazon's Umbro shorts were riding up her beefy thighs, almost revealing a glimpse of her big nasty. Dear heavens. She was alongside a youngster, and they were running right toward me. It was Little Bully and his angry looking mother. She looked like she was going to wallop me. I was convinced she was planning to flatten me like a steamroller. I hopped up and grabbed Jordan.

"Ben...Max!" I yelled. "Time to go. Grab the ball! Let's move!"

I could see my gray minivan in the front row of the parking lot. Fortunately, Big Red was not fast. We had plenty of time to make it. Everyone was staring at us. I was glad that at least I'd have witnesses if she crushed my bones.

I lifted the stroller with one hand, and hollered at the boys one more time to get the ball and go. Surprisingly, they listened and came running after me. They must have noticed that I was panicking. They normally don't come the first ten times I call them. The eleventh time is our charm.

The cavewoman was breathing heavy and had to rest her knees. I could only assume that weight lifting was her forte, but cardio...not so much. She was panting, literally panting. I could see her long pinkish tongue from across the park. She was special.

"Stay right there!" she yelled. "I'll call da police!"

Are you fucking kidding me? For what? What a fool. Everyone was watching and some even had out their phones, recording it. I really know how to keep a low profile. Who the hell gets themselves into these kinds of messes? I decided to try and communicate with the Sasquatch.

"Your son is mean!" I yelled and approached my van. I was searching my bag for keys. I knew I had only minutes, if that, to find them.

"Whatchoo do to my chil'?" she yelled.

I wanted to tell her that the word *child* typically has the letter "d" on the end. I didn't say it though. I just kept fumbling for my keys and hoping that by some miracle she'd get shit on by a bird, and then she'd have to retreat. I knew that I was going to be a goner if I didn't find those fucking keys. She was starting to run again. She would reach me in seconds. That bottomless shit pit from hell bag I carry with me, had failed me once again. Fucking bag. Fucking keys.

Her cheeks were red and she was far too sweaty for such a breathtakingly gorgeous day. She was older than I suspected. In fact, up close, you could see how much smaller her bottom section was than her top. It appeared the only exercises she knew how to perform must have been limited to bench pressing and bicep curls. Well, that's still more than I do. She frightened me. Her yellow teeth and freckled, wrinkled skin looked like abstract art, because of none of what I saw on her face was proportionate, none of it. She was one angry old bird. She made it to my van, and when she did, I said a prayer and thanked the Lord that I wasn't her toothbrush. I couldn't imagine having to touch the inside of her mouth. Saliva stuck to her canine teeth as she opened her winded pipes to speak. One would think spending what had to be a lot of time on strengthening one's upper body muscles, that oral health would be of some priority. Not in her case.

"Listen here you little bitch, I am going to call the police on you if you don't..." she began.

All three boys were cowering safely behind me and that very moment, I finally found my keys. I didn't want to be body slammed while trying to strap the kids in, so I did the only thing a normal person would do at that moment. I looked her in her squinty, puffy eyes and I hit the panic button on my minivan key.

BEEP beep BEEP beep BEEP beep BEEP beep BEEP beep BEEP beep BEEP beep BEEP

The noise was deafening, but I needed to get her away. My kids were scared shitless. But it seemed to work. She backed up. She backed her ass up onto the curb. What now biatch? Who's the queen of the park now? I felt so superbly strong. I had the urge to throw a gang sign, but I don't know any, so I just made a peace sign and then I immediately felt stupid because I realized that it wasn't at all appropriate, considering the circumstances.

She continued to holler something over the noise. All I could make out was the word, "ball." What could she be trying to say? I strapped my kids in as the panic sound kept blaring. Finally it was my turn to get in the car. I walked to the driver's side and opened my door. The minute I did, the noise stopped. It must have been an automatic thing. As I was getting into my seat, I heard what she had been hollering.

"Give us back our ball!" she yelled, sounding angrier than a hornet.

"It's not your ball!" I said. "It's our ball!"

A whole swarm of people were watching this fiasco.

"Yeah," said Ben. "We have two of them."

At that moment a flood of heat came over me, I was blushing and actually emitting heat through my skin. Ben held up identical maroon-colored kickballs, one in each hand. I realized, oh shit, we don't have two of them! We must have left ours in the car. Damnit! It *was* their fucking ball. Well, sonofabitch. I made the split decision to reverse that minivan right out of the parking lot without returning the kickball. I know it was wrong, but I'm chalking it up to the fact that what I did, really took some balls.

~Vada

Thought for the Day

What the hell is wrong with people? That's all.

A Goodnight Poem, by Vada Bower

My sweet darling angel love
Whatever is the matter?
A precious voice has woke me
With some precious baby chatter
I tried to let you work it out
I tried to let you be
But then your coos turned into wails
Oh honey don't you see?
Mommy needs some fucking sleep
I'm tired and I'm cold
I love your midnight waking
But this shit is getting old
What can I do to help you child?
May I sing you a song?
I'll buy you anything you want
If you'll sleep all night long
Now rest your head my little lamb
No arguments or buts
Your dad is sound asleep again
I'd like to crush his nuts
Dream about a kitty cat
Dream of a speckled pup
Hell, lay there if you want awake
But please shut the fuck up
I love you so much little one
Even though you woke
But please quit acting wide awake
You're not on fucking coke
So here's your little blankie
And here's your binky too
Now shut your precious fucking mouth
My baby, I love you...

Pedicure Day

Mom came over today and handed me a gift card to the nail shop. I think it's called Passion Nails, or something like that. The name, for some reason, makes me think of blood streaks down some perverted sadistic billionaire's back, but that is neither here nor there. Mom thought I needed some help with my piggies and told me that I shouldn't "let myself go." I wasn't sure quite how to take that comment, but being as though I hadn't had a minute to myself in a while, I decided to go for it.

I get so intimidated going into those places! I'm not a "regular" and I never know what to do. For example, should I walk in and sit down, and wait for someone to acknowledge me? Should I look for a clipboard to sign my name on? What if I look for one but there isn't one, so then everyone wonders what the hell I am looking for, and they laugh at me when they figure it out because they know I'm looking for something that doesn't even exist? What if the nail technicians think I'm gross and then they all go in the back room and fight about who has to do my pedicure? What if whoever is doing it, talks about how gross my feet are out loud in a language that I don't understand, and I sit there totally oblivious and smiling like an ugly baby who doesn't know that they're ugly? What if I look like a fool? What if I have toe jam?

After quickly shaving my ankles and toes to ensure there were no little hairs, I swallowed my anxiety, picked up a large Diet Coke at the drive-thru, and went to get my piggies pampered. I walked in, picked an orangey-pinkish color, and was guided to the pedi chair without much fuss. I stuck my feet in the warm blue bubbly water. There were no other customers at that time. Phew! That was easier than I thought. The drop dead gorgeous Asian woman who greeted me, handed me a magazine, and pulled up the tray on the side of the chair so that I could set my Diet Coke on it. It reminded me of a hospital tray, but it served its purpose. The room was peaceful, and some early 90's music was playing on the speakers overhead. Hey, the music could have been much worse. Things were going well. She walked away and let me soak for a minute. After seeing how put together she looked, it made me wish I would have at least made an effort to look cute today. My ponytail and "barely there makeup" made me feel insecure. I didn't even think about what my face and hair looked like when I was rushing out the door. I was too worried about the porcupine quills growing out of my toes and ankles. To make matters worse, three college age girls came bouncing in and were being seated by other employees.

All three of them were blonde and they reeked of confidence. They talked too loud and acted like no one could hear them. I knew in reality they just wanted everyone to hear their conversations about their carefree, shallow, and egocentric lives. Maybe at 31, I am too old for that shit, but I wanted to tell them that I don't fucking care which guy took them home from the party last night, or which slut jeans they wanted to go buy after they left. I just didn't fucking care...and neither did the ladies that were doing their nails, so they should have really considered lowering their goddamn voices a couple of fucking decibels, because I was just about to roll up my magazine, walk over, and smack them in their stupid mouths. Even though they were obnoxious, I did try to see what colors they chose, but only to make sure I was on trend. I wasn't. They all chose different shades of purple. Bitches.

Miss Pretty Face nail lady came back and sat on her bench. She started to work lotion into my neglected feet and ankles. Why couldn't this lady have looked like a hamster? Why did she have to have on lipstick? What do people do all day, just sit in front of the mirror and make themselves look nice?

Suddenly, she stopped what she was doing, and looked up at me with a face that could make a Disney princess look like a haggard old troll. "What happen to your toe?" she asked.

Oh fuck. I thought everyone had seen webbed toes before. They're not uncommon. So what? I have a little webbing between my second and third toe. To me this looks completely normal. I don't even stop to think about it. That is, until some beautiful nail tech points it out. Why'd she have to mention it? Did she think she was revealing to me some deformity that I never knew I had? Could she be that mean, that she just wanted me to feel embarrassed? I can't stand judgment, especially when I'm already anxious to begin with. At that point I wanted to leave. Not only did I feel ugly in my face, but this lady was literally holding my flaws in the palm of her hand. I wanted to tell her that there was nothing that "happened" to my toes. I wanted to say, "Hey, you know what? It's a long story, but my father is actually a ring-necked mallard that lives down at the pond. He went down south for the winter but should be back when things warm up a bit. My mother had an insatiable lust for waterfowl. In fact, have you ever heard the expression, *well fuck a duck*? Yeah, some people do it, and then their babies come out just like this. Quack quack bitch."

I mean, how dare this stunning little goddess insult me? I sat there, not sure of what to do next. I was speechless. So, I did the only thing any sane person would have done in that moment of mortification. I reached for my purse to grab a Xanax. Only, upon doing this, my elbow hit the tray and my delicious fountain drink went tumbling down to the ground, but not without splashing all over my shirt and lime-green sweats with the hiked-up elastic hems, that I thought were perfect pedicure pants. I immediately apologized and stepped out of the water. Miss Pretty Face ran for towels. She handed me one and we worked together to clean up the mess. The college girls were staring at me. Two of them had their hands over their mouths. I knew they were trying not to laugh. I actually couldn't blame them. It got even better. I stood up so quickly that I hit my stupid head on the tray that my coke had been on. It didn't hurt really, but it made a loud noise and added to my embarrassment, while also adding to the three little college skanks' amusement.

"You okay?" asked Miss Pretty Face.

"Just fine. I'm sorry. I have...a...a...AIDS," I said. It came out in slow motion like in a movie, when the actor's voice turns deep and the audio is dragged out.

Why would I have said that? It was the first thing I could think of. I don't

196

have AIDS. I don't even have HIV. Hell, I don't even have a cold! I do however, freak out in times of stress. Besides, having AIDS doesn't make someone spill drinks and act like a looney tune. My words got mixed up. All I do know is, when making an excuse, "I have a..." can easily be turned into something catastrophic if you don't know what word you're going to put after the "a."

I was ready to scream. I grabbed my purse, handed the beauty a twenty-dollar bill, slipped on my non-weather appropriate flip-flops, thanked her, and told her I had to go. I actually told her that I had a meeting. WTF? Where would my meeting have possibly been? The AIDS clinic?

I got into my minivan and was overcome with relief, quite similar to the relief one feels when finally being able to break wind after a long and quiet dinner with the in-laws. I leaned down to return the elastic hem of my hiked-up pants back to my ankle, and that's when I saw it: a trail of blood running down by big toe. Well, fuck me on a steep hill. At that moment, I realized what Miss Pretty Face had meant when she asked what happened to my toe. I realized I must have cut it during my quick shave. I can only imagine what Miss Pretty Face was thinking inside that nail salon at that moment. What a calamity. What a disaster. I should never leave my house.

I stopped at the drug store on the way home and bought a bag of chocolate-covered peanuts and some purple nail polish. I painted my pigs in the parking lot. I wasn't even going to attempt explaining to my mother why I had come home with unpedicured feet.

Note to self, purple is not your color Vada.

Here's a Thought...

Since life gets so busy with birthday parties, sports, playdates, etc...I thought I would start a family calendar to keep track of all our events. So two weeks ago, I started it. It's a great big ol' bastard, with a clip-on pen and everything. I hung it on the refrigerator so that we could just jot things down whenever they happened to come up.

Two weeks later, I have found that none of the shit we have going on, has even been written on the calendar. The reason is simple: If I am so busy that I have to start writing down every single thing that has to be done, then I certainly don't have the time to fucking write it all down. In order to do that, it would require me to have to be firmly planted in my kitchen next to my fridge at all times, preferably with the pen in my hand. Who does that? Who has time for that? Stupid calendar. Stupid idea. I need to go get a Diet Coke, and I'm not putting that on the calendar.

Cuckoo Cuckoo

So as a tool, call it a bribe if you want, I have been using a sticker reward chart with my precious angels to encourage good behavior. Basically, I'm trying to keep them from their bad behaviors which include, but are not limited to: ripping off each other's faces, pulling out their junk to take a piss on every patch of grass they see, and saying bad words. I have no clue where they would have heard bad words. Last week, they earned ten stickers each and were rewarded with a trip to see an awful animated movie at the theater. They loved it, I hated it, everyone who mattered won. Now what reward did I use this week? Let me tell you:

While walking through a sporting goods store the other day, Ben took a fancy to these little do-it-yourself birdhouses. It was an all-in-one kit; complete with a hanger, a set of paintbrushes, and five colors of paint, all for the bargain price of $16.99. Clearly the price doubled as I have two children old enough for this project, and in good conscience, I could not purchase just one. This brought the potential purchase grand pre-tax total to $33.98. I told my minions that if they earned ten more stickers, then I would take them to buy birdhouses.

Guess who earned those stickers like a couple of bosses? That's right. So, I got up this morning and thought to myself, *I bet I could go to Hobby Lobby and find birdhouses and paint supplies there at a much cheaper price.* We loaded in the car, picked up my antidepressants at the pharmacy, stopped for a large Diet Coke with extra ice, and went to America's favorite hobby store. Once again, I must give myself credit. Making birdhouses? Ha! I should be one of those Pinterest bitches.

Once we got inside the store, I sat Jordan in the front of the awkwardly small cart. Such cute home décor sidetracked me into browse-mode. I found an adorable piece of wooden wall art that looked like a worn white picket fence for $34.99, which I absolutely had to have. In fact, I knew that if I didn't have it, the sun might burnout and the world would end due to a devastating, global ice age. I placed it in the cart, but there was no way it would fit in that tiny basket unless I took Jordan out and closed the seat.

So, I did. I let him walk, and tried to hold his hand and push the cart at the same time. Yeah, that was fun.

The boys began to get grabsy. Max picked up a red glass ball off the shelf and began to yell, "Look at these big balls!" Ben was frustrated that he could not turn on any of the lamps that were not plugged in, and that was my signal to quit browsing and find the damn birdhouses. We made it a little further back in the store, when the inevitable happened.

"I gotta go to the bathroom!" Max said and he was crouched down on the floor like the tiger from hidden dragon. The way he doubled over let me know that we had to move fast, or this could end with a call for a clean-up in aisle 32.

I looked around, and much to my delight, the restrooms were nestled directly in the rear of the store only about thirty feet away.

"Alright nuggets, let's go hit the toilets," I said.

Jordan stopped instantly in his tracks, looked directly into my eyes, smiled so sweetly you would have thought an angel from above had just kissed his chubby little cheek, and then he took off like a bat out of hell down through the wearable art aisle. Bolting after him in my purple cotton sundress I finally caught up, and carried the little animal kicking and screaming back to where our cart was and straight into the bathroom.

I found an empty stall. In true Vada-style, I doctored up the toilet seat with tissue for Max's delicate bottom and hoisted him up to do his work. I can't stand the thought of him touching anything. I keep the kids very close to me in public restrooms so that they will not touch anything. I may not get away with this much longer though, as they are getting older and it may look weird one day to have teenagers holding onto me in the bathroom.

The worst thing though, in a public restroom with kids, is that when they're on the toilet, their pants can touch the floor, or even the front of the bowl, where people's stray hairs or drips have fallen. Keep in mind, these drips can be from so many disgusting things that thinking about it makes my butt cheeks clinch and my toes curl. Anyway, Jordan decided to play the fussy, difficult toddler and was clinging to me for dear life. Ben was instructed to stay right behind me and not touch anything.

I know that Jordan feeds off my anxiety, and I was trying to calm him down. At the same time, I was doing my best to ensure that Max didn't let his skin touch the porcelain. While trying to juggle those two difficult tasks, and thinking of quite a colorful list of words in my mind, I felt a warm trickling sensation on my neck. Max had forgotten to push his wiener down and his urine stream was now running down the front of my throat and into my cleavage. I screamed and jumped to the side, accidentally leaving Ben in the line of fire. Max's arching stream then landed all over Ben's ankles, and his black and green Skechers light-ups. In a panic, I took charge and pushed Max's unit down. It was too late, he was finished; numbers one and two. He was laughing hysterically. I'm not kidding, he was cracking up. Ben was not. Ben was pissed, quite literally for that matter.

Trying not to lose my cool, I reminded myself that children who witness violent outbursts are more likely to have anger issues as adults. With that in mind, I took the boys to the sinks. Ben was now crying and I couldn't blame him. Having your brother give you a golden shower is a tragic experience. I wiped his shoes off with soapy paper towels and begged him to calm down. After everyone's hands were scrubbed, I wanted to leave, but I did not come this far to leave empty handed. We had some birdhouses to buy.

Ben was still incredibly upset, so I thought I would distract him by showing him some of those model cars they always have in hobby stores, because he fucking loves cars. He and Max each found one they wanted and they were "buy one, get one half off," so they ended up being $29.98 together. I was desperate. I let them have them. We finally made it to the unfinished wood aisle. I found two birdhouses that each came in a box, and they were on sale for $6.04 apiece. I hurriedly read the instructions and now had to purchase wood glue - $2.50, plus sandpaper - $2.75, plus paint - $4.00, plus paintbrushes, which were $4.00 for a small bag. Fuck that's a lot of shit. I took the kids and headed straight for the counter to pay, but not before bumping into a clock shaped like a John Deere tractor, and knocking the minute hand off.

There were two lines, both were doing price checks. One of the obnoxious price checks was for an elderly woman with an ugly picture frame, and one was for a wreath I could have made in my backyard, being purchased by a lady whose shorts were so short she could probably taste them in her mouth. All I wanted to do was spear them both with a sharpened stick. I mean, did I really look like I had time for this shit? The boys were starting to scatter. I lured them back with a bag of gummy bears, $1.50. After sorting out the pricing issues with the previous customers, the cashier looked at me and said, "Oh, I guess you've waited long enough haven't you? I saw you guys in the bathroom."

I was unaware that anyone else was even in the bathroom, so her comment caught me by surprise, but I laughed my fake laugh and said, "Oh yes, it's just one of those days."

The bitch stared back at me and said, "I understand. I have a little girl at home."

Really? That comment she made, meant I actually had to restrain myself from sticking her price checker up her ass in search of a barcode. That's like telling someone with severe acne that you feel like you're getting a zit. It took all of my self-control not to say, "Lady, do you smell piss in here? Because that would be me. Has your daughter ever pissed on your neck? Oh no? Really? Then shut the fuck up."

Anyway, we made it out to the car without assault charges, and as I looked down at my receipt I realized the my "price saving" adventure cost me $91.80 plus tax, instead of the $33.98 I would have spent on the original pre-assembled birdhouses.

Fucking hell, that's what I get for trying to be thrifty. I better get to bed, because tomorrow I've got to put these stupid model cars together, and figure out what to do with this giant piece of white picket fence. And one more thing; I have to make a trip to the store to buy birdseed and purchase something for Jordan out of guilt, because he didn't get anything. Oh Vada, you crazy bitch...

BAM I'm like magic

So...today I had an epiphany. Every time I take the baby out in public, I have terrible anxiety over whether or not he will crap his pants and have to have his diaper changed on a public changing table. I used to buy cheap blankets to lay him down on, and then throw them away, because the thought of another baby's fecal issues in my diaper bag, doesn't fly with my OCD. I will no longer waste that much money, and I will ease my own stress. I have found a solution. I went to the pet store today and bought puppy training pads. BAM! I amaze myself. Cheap, disposable, and clean. I can lay them from end to end on the changing table, and my little baby boy doesn't have to be covered from head to toe with E. coli. Why did it take me until my third child to figure this out? Today I've conquered the changing table...tomorrow, who knows?

Confessions about today...

1. I dropped Ben and Max off at school, and then when I got home, I realized that I forgot to send Ben's homework folder with him. It's one that I have to sign and return so his teacher can see that I looked at it. So, I emailed his teacher and blamed it on Eric. I even made a joke about how you can't trust a man to do anything.

2. Eric called me from work and asked what I was doing, and I was really laying on the couch watching a *Real Housewives* rerun, but I acted like I was out of breath and told him I had just vacuumed the stairs.

3. A man came to the door selling pest control services and I told him my parents weren't home.

4. I pulled up to the drive-thru at McDonalds after picking the boys up from school. The kids were all really into the movie that was playing on the DVD player. I was only going for a Diet Coke, I swear, but since no one was paying attention, I ordered an ice cream cone and held it close to my chest and no one ever found out. It was delicious.

5. I ate a lot of taco meat and a few handfuls of cheese while I was cooking supper. I ate so much of it in fact, that I was full by the time I put dinner on the table. Then, I lied and told Eric I was on a diet and that's why I wasn't eating.

Cliques

Sometimes, I think that being the mother of an elementary-schooler comes with more peer pressure than high school. When I go to pick up the boys and I walk up to the parents' waiting area, who do I stand by? Where do I fit in? Am I going to be the anti-social one who stands there with no one to talk to? Will these women accept me as part of their peer group, or will I be ostracized and made to stand there waiting all alone, listening to the friendly surface conversations of the mothers around me who actually fit in? I need a benzo just thinking about it.

First of all, there are the moms who are always dressed up. These are the women who are dressed up because they are just getting off work. They look so important. I like them all, I really do. It's just that it can be intimidating. I mean, here they all just left their careers where they have to do real career-type shit. I most likely have just scrubbed a toilet, or have a booger on my shirt. Also, many of them are in heels. This makes me feel almost inferior, most likely because I'm incredibly short to begin with, and in flats, and yes, probably have a booger on my shirt.

Then there are the fitness moms. These are the ones who show up in their spandex situations each and every day, looking like their BMI could kick my BMI's ass, and even though their hair is pulled back, it looks adorable. I like these ladies and would love to be one of them. It's just that I fucking HATE working out. Plus, Jordan doesn't let me work out during the day. He doesn't even let me piss. So maybe this isn't the group for me. Although I must admit, I have worn workout clothes just to give the impression that I work out, but they all know better I'm sure. I mean, if I really would have been out running, would I always be in flip-flops? I don't think so.

Then, there are what I like to call, the mirror moms. These are the ones who don't necessarily work outside the home, but who wear actual real clothes and full makeup. They have their hair down and styled, and look like they are ready for a big date. But in reality, they are doing the same shit that I am. It's just that *I* actually look like I've been doing it. I admire the ladies that put on jewelry to pick up their kids, but I can't keep up. I'm lucky if my hair gets washed, let alone dried and curled into romantic waves. They are usually very friendly, but holy shit, I don't want to stand next to them. It's like, what's my excuse? If they can keep themselves presentable, why can't I? I don't need that fucking pressure in my life. Shit, I'm just trying to get to pick-up on time.

There are several other groups as well, like the super-involved and competitive dads, and the parents, both male and female, who bring their dogs every day, so they can stand there and let their dogs sniff each others' asses.

There are also the prairie women, who each have a ton of kids, and I expect they will yank their children out of the public education system at any moment in order to home school them.

Let's not forget the socially phobic moms. These are the ones who cower down like you are going to elbow them in the face immediately after you offer a friendly, "hi" and then they find a new place to stand. I actually kind of like these bitches. They don't even pretend to like you. They just stay the hell away.

I guess I don't fit in after all. I may start my own clique. It's going to be something like this: The moms who wear clothes you could work out in, but they never actually work out, who also have bags under their eyes because they have crazy kids who don't sleep, and who sometimes wear makeup, but most of the time just wear big sunglasses so that no one will know they haven't looked in the mirror yet today. I'm going to seek out these moms and make sure I stand by them. I guess that means tomorrow at pick-up, I'll scout out the three moms who look most likely to have just smoked crack.

If for some reason, I can't find my place on the social ladder, and I find there is no one out there willing to accept me, I'll resort to standing by my lonesome. I'll take some comfort in knowing that no matter how alone I feel, I've always got my crazy, and no one can take that away from me. No one.

The truth about my OCD

Eric, and only a few of my friends, know good and well that I have OCD. It always cracks me up when people are like, "I have OCD, so I have to make lists," or "I'm so OCD that I have to keep things in their places." I'm like, really? Do you have to make lists and then read them three times, because if you don't you'll be up all night with racing thoughts including one where you will literally choke on your own saliva, swallow your tongue, and die right there in your bed if the list does not get read for a third fucking time? Oh no? Then you don't have OCD.

I know it's a slang term these days, and some people actually do have OCD tendencies, so I don't get offended, and I rarely judge, unless they're just idiots. I'm no doctor; it's not my call to make. But I have true OCD; the kind where I count shit and repeat words in my head a certain number of times. I have a horrible time with odd numbers. I also have a problem with dirty floors to the point that I have every kind of mop, broom, robotic floor duster, spray, polish, and carpet cleaner, ever made. I mop three times a day, even if it doesn't need it. I know the number three is an odd number and I hate it, but three is also one of my hang up numbers, meaning I do most of my compulsions three times. My floors look good, but are never clean enough. I bet my neighbors look through the windows and think I am always humping the floor. I'm always down with one eye open, checking for stray hairs or mystery particles. It's a struggle, but I can't help it.

This one's a doozy; if there is a shower curtain in the bathroom, I have to open and close it three times. If I have to pee, I leave it open. I try my best to avoid places with shower curtains at all costs. I can't help but assume, that watching me walk down the home bath aisle in a department store, has to be somewhat similar, to watching a teenage girl in one of those downtown haunted houses.

Well shit! Writing this down makes me realize that I definitely have issues. I'm not done either. When I drive, or am riding in a car, I have to bite down half-way between fence posts, driveways, and light poles. Usually no one notices. It's very subtle. Most of the time, I don't even realize that I am doing it, especially if I am nervous (which actually is most of the time). I used to turn faucets on and off three times, but somehow, and I don't know why, that one stopped in my teens. WTF? I freak myself out. But you know what? Even though I hate the number three because it is odd, there is one wonderful thing about it. I have my three boys. So, when I start to get bothered by these things that seem like roadblocks for me in my life, I sometimes wonder if they are there for a reason, leading me where I need to go. Having my boys made me realize that.

At least, that's what I tell myself to keep me from feeling so batshit crazy. Whatever works.

Night, Night, Night.
~Vada

Positive thinking

I am really going to try to start being a more positive person. I hate when things seem so negative and draining in my life. When the kids want a snack, I'm not going to complain in my head about having to stop what I am doing and go into the kitchen. I'm not going to get pissy when I offer them like fifty fucking delicious choices and they turn everything down, and then ask what else we have to eat. I am not going to growl when they choose a messy as hell yogurt tube instead of neat and tidy Goldfish crackers. I'm certainly not going to make a sour face when the yogurt ends up being squeezed too hard and gushes out of the tube, and onto their hands, all over the table, and then drips onto my freshly mopped floor, where they try to clean it up with a dish towel, so I won't notice, and end up just spreading it all over the damn place, and I catch them in the act and then I have to wash the towel. There's no way I'm going to roll my eyes when I have to remove their outfits and use Spray 'n Wash to soak the strawberry pink stains so that they won't set in and ruin their clothes. You won't catch me griping when I have to give them baths because I can't handle sticky things, and then they dump water out all over the floor, and now I have even more towels to wash. I won't say one bad thing when I go back to clean up the table and floor catastrophe that they failed to clean properly the first time, and so then I have to re-mop it using the scrubbing strip because it has begun to dry. Nope, I won't say a word. You won't hear a peep from me once I finally get everything cleaned up from all of the yogurt, (that didn't even make it into their mouths), and they come back up to me with big innocent eyes, and they smile ever so sweetly and ask me for another motherfucking snack, because they are still fucking hungry since their previous snack barely made into their mouths. I will still remain positive. In fact, I'm going to smile while I give them a new snack and then kiss their little faces. Then, I am going to get on my knees and thank the Lord for my happy pills because without them, I would have gone full-blown flip my shit psycho by now, and I'm totally *positive* about that.

Random Rules to Live By:

1. If you find yourself cheating on a diet, just eat your guilt-ridden and scrumptious contraband as fast as you possibly can and then forget about it. Quit living in the past.

2. When someone asks you if you want to hang out on Friday, start coughing right that second. It will set up the scenario later that you are sick and simply cannot hang out when Friday rolls around.

3. Teach your children to not only accept their peers who are different from themselves, but to seek out these children and make friends with them. Not only will it keep your kids from becoming douchey assholes, but it can add value and happiness to their lives, as children with differences can have a whole hell of a lot to offer.

Cock-a-doodle-doo

When I woke up this morning, I realized that for the first time in ages, my kids had slept all night in their beds. This was such a victory. I can't remember the last time they did that. They must have been really tired.

Upon waking, I sat up and squinted while leaning across Eric to see the digital alarm clock, which without my contacts, looked like brake lights fishtailing at nighttime. It was only six o'clock. Being as this was a Saturday morning, I was super stoked to hunker down and go back to sleep, hoping everyone would sleep in. Hallelujah, it was finally happening!

Then I felt it. I felt it right where you feel it when the gentlemen spoons you. It was Eric and his morning wood. What the hell is his cock so happy for this early in the morning? What is he, a rooster or something? Shit, he saw me lean over and he knew I was awake. Now, he was poking me with that thing of his. I tried to breathe heavy like I was falling back asleep, and was totally ignoring his humping motions. Don't you think after five minutes of no response, he'd get a clue? Nope. Not Mr. Pokey. He kept pecking me with it.

I opened my eyes, turned over and said, "Listen here, you pervert, unless you plan on rubbing my back with that thing, then keep it to yourself. I'm trying to sleep here!"

That motherfucker must have thought I was kidding. He just kept at it and then put a hand on my boob. I rolled over on my stomach and crossed my legs real tight, completely blocking every point of entry. He just kept going. He was trying to pry my legs open like he was using the jaws of life without saying a word. It's like my body language wasn't enough. All I ever wanted was to sleep. Is that too much to ask?

"Come on, why do you shut me down?" he asked.

"Because I would rather have massive diarrhea in a port-a-potty in the middle of August at a cockfight in Mexico City then to have sex right now," I growled.

"You're not going to turn me off, so quit trying," he said.

"I'm not trying to turn you off. I am just telling the truth, so leave me alone. I really want to sleep. Just go in the bathroom and play with it if you need to, but leave me alone."

"Vada, it likes you. Just let it come in, at least just the tip."

"No, and you sound like a disgusting pervert. Now get it away from me and keep it on your side of the bed! Besides, I wouldn't even kiss you right now. I haven't even brushed my teeth."

"It doesn't care what your breath smells like," he said and tried to make a move with his hand on my girl bottom.

At that moment, I just lost it. I kicked and flailed all over the bed, like a child who didn't want to wake up for school. I was pissed and tired. I could care less about his Willy Wonka. I just wanted to be left alone! This attack had lasted at least forty-five minutes of precious sleeping time. I hopped up from the bed, grabbed a Batman blanket that Max had left in our room, and went down to the couch, so I could be left in peace. He knew better than to follow me. I am not a morning person. Nestled on the big comfy beige sectional, I curled up in a ball and closed my eyes. The very moment I felt myself drifting off, little footsteps hauled ass down the hallway. Instead of heading to my bedroom, they stopped. Fucking hell, I'd been spotted. Next time, I'll go sleep on the deck.

"Mommy, I'm hungry!" yelled Max.

"And I'm thirsty," said Ben right behind him.

"Mammmmmmma!" I heard coming from Jordan's closed bedroom door.

Goddamnit! They woke up Jordan. I knew I had to get up now. What a waste of my time trying to sleep in. Stupid Eric had ruined it all for me. If he would have just left me alone, I would have been able to sleep until seven o'clock for the first time in over a year. Fuck him!

So I got Jordan out of his crib, sat him in his chair with some Cheerios, and began to make breakfast, which was pancakes and bacon. The kids were watching Saturday morning cartoons and it was just another day at the Bower house. This is, until Eric emerged from our bedroom door, which I could see from the kitchen. You're not going to fucking believe what happened next.

He rubbed his eyes and stood there with his shirt off. He gave me that pouty look he gives, and said this, "Hey, would you mind keeping the kids quiet? I'd really like to sleep another hour if that's okay with you. I don't know why, but I'm really tired."

Are you fucking kidding me? I stood there thinking that it's a good damn thing he was so far away from me, because I would have burnt him with bacon grease.

"Sure," I said, not wanting to fight in front of the kids.

Eric shut the door and I waited for a few minutes.

I lifted the kids' finished breakfast off the griddle onto their plastic Spiderman plates. Then, I dressed their pancakes up with butter and syrup. They all got their juice and gummy vitamins to go along with their classic breakfast. I was feeling like a Supermom. I hate to cook, so a hot breakfast is kind of a big deal for me. After taking my sweet time with the kids, I went back and checked on the now burnt black bacon and hockey puck pancakes that I had left on the griddle. Perfect! I pulled them off, put them on a plate, and set the plate on a tray with silverware, along with my cup of coffee that had now gone cold. It wasn't quite complete. I reached into the pantry, found a bottle of cider vinegar and dumped a few capfuls into the coffee. Voila! Now it was ready. Once the kids had their bellies full, I gathered them around for a meeting.

"Boys," I said, "Daddy had a hard week at work, so I want you to run in my room and yell, "Surprise!" as loud as you can, okay? Then jump all over him and wake him up because we have breakfast in bed all ready for him! I know I cooked it, but it's the thought that counts. The surprise is the biggest part, so go in and scream as loud as you can, right in his face. "

Oh they were thrilled. So excitedly, they ran up the steps and did exactly as I had asked. I fucking love it when they listen! It sounded like the screaming lambs from Clarice's childhood. Fuck yeah! I could hear Eric groaning. Then, I came up the stairs with an ear-to-ear smile while singing in an awful opera voice, "Its breaaaaaakfast tiiiiiiiime for Daaaaaaaddy!"

Eric sat up looking like he'd been beaten in the head with a sledge hammer, and I set the tray on his lap.

"Thanks guys," he said. "That's so nice of you." He was giving me a puzzled look, which I ate up like Thanksgiving dinner.

"You better eat your breakfast Daddy," I said.

"Yeah Daddy," said Max. "We know you had a hard week. This will make you feel better."

"Better eat Daddy, the boys really wanted to surprise you," I said sincerely.

Eric just sat there and stared at the burnt to a crisp mess in front of him. He knew he had to eat it so it wouldn't hurt the boys' feelings. I'm sure it was as awful as it looked. My favorite part, was when he spit his vinegar coffee back into the cup and then looked around for a non-existent secondary beverage to rinse his mouth with. I had to laugh out loud when he sprang from the bed to wash his mouth in the bathroom sink. Sucker. I stood at the end of the bed with my arms crossed and celebrated my victory. All in all, I think he learned his lesson.

Revenge is a motherfucker. Maybe next time, he'll think twice before trying to fuck with this mother. Now I'm going to bed, and I am soooo sleeping in tomorrow.

Confessions about today...

1. I was too lazy to do laundry, so I just restarted the washer so that the wet clothes wouldn't get sour.

2. My phone rang and I didn't want to answer it, so I froze completely still as if somehow that would keep the caller from knowing I was home. Then I kept looking out the window in fear that this person was in the area and would stop by and realize that I wasn't busy, I was just avoiding their call.

3. I got an instant message on Facebook and I immediately logged off because I have anxiety about "chatting."

4. I turned on the radio in the car and heard the song, *Ditty*. I was singing along full force when I came to a stop at a red light. Next to me was an extended-cab pickup filled with construction workers who were actually kind of foxy. I was really embarrassed and afraid they witnessed my jam session, so I held a finger up to my ear and pretended like I was talking into a Bluetooth.

5. I tried to twerk in my kitchen all by myself, just to see if I could do it, and I think I can. So there.

The Plague

I've been up for over thirty-six hours and I'm not even sure what I'm writing here. In fact, I'm not even sure that I'm alive. Maybe I'm in limbo, caught between dimensions. I feel like I've been beaten with a club and have a concussion. This is because our home has been struck by the bubonic plague, aka *Influenza A*. We have dropped like flies, and for some reason, even though I have it as well, no one cares about dear ol' mommy. I may as well jump out in front of a fucking truck. I could be bleeding out every hole in my body, and the family would expect me to wait on them hand and foot. We didn't get our flu shots. Of course that's my fault too. I'm a bad mom. I'm so tired. I have $300 worth of Tamiflu sitting in the fridge. What's the point now? It's too late. For $300, if I'm going to buy medicine, it better take me to Wonderland and I better be able to smoke that shit. I know if I go to sleep one of those kids is going to wake up. I want to boil water and scald Eric while he's sleeping. He's been asleep for ten hours now. My kids are staggering their sleeping shifts. They just wake up crying.

I'm too sick to sleep and the chills are killing me. My mind is racing. How do women possibly stand having vaginal lifts? Wouldn't that hurt? I mean, I get that their roast beef is spilling out of the sandwich, but to cut it off? Oh good gracious. If mine ever got like that, I'd just roll it up and tuck it in, and then cover it with duct tape. I'm so tired. I think my fever is making me delirious. Even my fingers hurt. If I don't wake up that means the flu has taken me in my sleep. I hope Eric is proud of himself. He's, "so sick I can't move." How does he think I feel? Plus, I'm taking care of three kids who are miserable. I wonder if people who eat sushi actually like it, or they just think it makes them look trendy. I mean, some people probably like it, but I bet some don't, but eat it anyway. It's like me with coffee drinks. I went through a phase where I'd go get a grande skinny double mocha ya ya frappe iced latte, or something like that, and it tasted awful, but I liked ordering it and then carrying it around with my keys in my hand like the celebs do in *Us Weekly*. This was in the pre-kid years. I got over it after I realized how many calories were in it, and how much money I was spending just to look hip. I'm hip without trendy drinks. You know what's fucking good? Kool-Aid, cherry effing Kool-Aid. I love when the sugar granules get stuck on my tongue. I'm so thirsty right now.

My fever is 102.1 and I think I want my mom. She cares about me...I think. I guess not that much though, because she's not here helping me. She said she doesn't want to get the flu. How selfish. Way to think of others grandma. Someday, when I'm spoon feeding her Jell-O and broths and such, I'll remind her of how she selfishly left me here to die in front of my children. Oh Lord, I hear something. It's Ben. He's yelling for me. Why can't they ever at least once, just once, yell for Eric? I know why. It's 'cause I am the shit and the kids know it. Okay, now I gotta go. God be with me.

The Double Date

The other night Eric asked me to go on a double date with him and his work buddy. Okay, why the hell not? I know this guy. His name is Ryan. He is single, attractive, and polite, and I had no reason to say no because my mother had already offered to let us have a night out. I was thinking dinner, a glass of wine or three or four, small talk that would turn into a new best friendship, that would result in us all vacationing together on three-day weekends. Not really, but I decided, what the hell? It's just one night. Except, then I found out where we were going. It was the Kansas City Royals game. Okay, I am a KC girl and I like the Royals, and baseball is fine and all, plus there are really good hot dogs, and pretzels with cheese, and beers. I like beers at ballgames. The only downside is that it's so noisy and I never get a minute of quiet, but on the bright side, we wouldn't have to make small talk and again, there would be beers. So I agreed.

The night came around and I threw on a pair of jeans and a blue and white baseball tee. I tossed my hair up in a ponytail and threw on some Nikes. I dabbed on my lip gloss and headed down to kiss the kids goodbye. My mother had come to watch the boys. I had to tell them we were going to the toilet store to shop for toilets, because they would have freaked if they knew we were going to a ballgame without them. I kissed each one of them, and Eric and I ran out the door. We were planning on meeting Ryan and his date in the parking lot for a drink before we went in.

We pulled into the stadium and after paying way too much to park, we found Ryan's BMW, and he and a pretty blonde were still sitting inside. Ryan's got money. He's got lots of money, so he usually finds some pretty young thing; a new one each time. I was expecting a cute girl to come out of that car. What I wasn't expecting however, was what *actually* came out of the car.

The black passenger door opened and I saw a foot step on to the ground. It wasn't just any foot though; it was a foot in a five-inch red stiletto with a gold ankle cuff, housing a bed of white-polished toenails. The second stiletto hit the pavement and up out of that luxury vehicle stood a lady as tall as a water tower. She was wearing a short black sleeveless dress with a gold statement necklace. Effing really? I was beginning to wonder if we were at the Grammy's. Her golden locks hung down past her decently-sized melons, and her arms were so long that if included her nails I would have bet that her wing-span could rival a pterodactyl's. Her blue eyes were sparkling with makeup and fake eyelashes. WTF? I thought we were at a ballgame? I looked up at her wondering if this was for real or if this was a joke.

"Hello, I'm Trinity," she leaned in and kissed my cheek on one side, and I was so scared I wanted to run. Then, she kissed my other cheek. I don't even get that much action out of Eric so I think I may have just cheated on him.

"I'm Vada," I said. I tried to act pleased to meet her. The guys were over doing the man "back slap hug" and had already popped open beers. I guess they just expected me and Trinity to automatically hit it off, and run out and buy best friend necklaces.

"Your name is Vada?" she asked. "Were you named after that girl on that movie? That movie with that girl named Vada? I think it was like *Your Girl*, or no...*My Girl*! Were you named after her?

Oh fuck me. I wanted to choke her. I wanted to tell her yes, that I was actually named Harriet when I was born, but when the movie came out in 1991 when I was ten, my parents just loved it so much, and they rushed me to the courthouse to legally change it. Stupid bitch.

"Actually, it was my great-grandmother's name. Her name was Nevada," I explained.

"That sounds like a state. So how did you get the nickname Vada?" she asked, twirling her hair.

I wanted to take her stiletto off and jam it into her temple. I seriously thought she was fucking with me. But no, she was just stupid.

"After *My Girl*," I said. I decided to just let her believe it. "Hey Eric, did you meet Trinity?" I hollered to the other side of the BMW.

Eric walked over and stretched out his hand. I was so relieved when she shook it because if they would have done the kissy-kissy thing, I think that would have meant that we just had a threesome. We had all exchanged pleasantries and now I was ready for a drink. If I had to stand next to this chick all night, I sure as hell needed some remedy to get me through it.

"Eric, grab me a beer kid, I need a swallers," I said. I was giving him that look. The look that meant, I will rip your balls off if you abandon me tonight.

"Oh Vada," said Trinity. "You should drink with me. I brought something better."

Confused, I asked, "What have you got?"

"I've got a Bald Pussy."

Holy biscuits and gravy, why was she telling me this? I didn't know what was wrong with this chick. She pulled out a handle of vodka but it was a weird green color. "It's so good - you have to try it. I mixed up a batch. It's all I drink anymore. It's a cocktail."

Oh thank the glorious stars! She was talking about the drink. That totally caught me by surprise. "I think I'd rather have a Busch," I said sarcastically.

"Eww...that's not good beer," she said. Oh my gracious, she was so dumb. She poured me a clear plastic cup full of the slightly green liquid, and then one for herself. I must admit this Bald Pussy tasted better than I thought it would. I headed over back over to Eric.

"What are you drinking?" he asked.

"Please don't ask," I said. I didn't want to give him any ideas.

We drank a little, then decided it was time to go in. I didn't want to get too drunk because then I wouldn't enjoy my ballpark food. I held Eric's hand and made sure we walked ahead of the glamour couple behind us. I had anxiety about having to sit by her, so I wanted to make sure that I was on the end. We finally found our seats and fortunately, I scurried into my spot. The game was just starting.

"You want anything to eat?" asked Eric.

"Umm...yeah. Get me a hotdog, and a pretzel and cheese. Oh and one more thing...cotton candy please."

"Okay hog," laughed Eric.

"You want anything?" Ryan asked Trinity.

"Oh, no thanks babe," she said all sexy like. "It's not on my fitness plan. Plus, I don't eat processed foods."

Babe? Really? Fitness plan? At a ballgame? All I could think of was how great it was that he found a girl who barely eats. I bet she doesn't shit either. What a gem. They kissed goodbye then Ryan and Eric went to fetch my buffet and their snacks.

I knew I was in for it then because she scooted down three seats to sit next to me. "So, do you think Ryan is really into me? I'm kind of ready to settle down," she said. I wondered if it was her Bald Pussy talking or if this girl was serious. I just met her. I would have liked for her to settle down too and get the hell away from me. I just smiled and pointed to the field like I couldn't hear a word she said. Thank goodness it was so loud. I managed to kill time clapping along with the songs and was just waiting for the "Kiss Cam" to come to us so she could smooch me again. Then I felt it, it was her hand. Her hand was on my face. She was turning my face to look at her. All

I could think was how many germs were on her hands. After touching railings walking in, and who knows what else. I tried not to be rude, so I didn't pull her hair like I wanted to. I just looked at her, hoping she'd get her fucking hands off my face.

"Vada, can you keep a secret?" she asked.

No. "Yeah sure, what is it?"

"I think I love Ryan."

I knew she loved his bank account. So do I. Hell, who wouldn't? "Well Trinity, that's just fantastic. Have you told him? I think you should tell him." I really wished she would tell him, so that when he came back, she'd be so busy professing her love to him that she'd leave me alone. I just met this girl. What the fuck did I care if she loved him or not?

"Ladies," said Ryan. He and Eric were back. I had hoped this bitch would move back to her spot so I could sit by Eric, but she didn't. He was three seats away from me, so I had to be handed my 5,000 calories down an assembly line. I grabbed my hand sanitizer and gave my fingers a good wash, then set my food out on my lap like I'd never eaten before. I just tried to get into the game, and let the couple next to me fall for each other. Suddenly, Trinity stood up.

"I'll be right back. I have to use the ladies room."

Her beautiful heeled-self pranced up the stairs, turning every guy's head. Part of me wondered if it was because she was so hot, or if she was just overdressed. Probably a little bit of both. I motioned Eric to come back and sit by me, and he obeyed.

"What the fuck's up with that chick's outfit?" he whispered in my ear. We both giggled. Ryan was staring at us.

"What do you think?" he asked.

"I think they're going to win!" I said, not even knowing what the score was.

"No," he said, "about Trinity?"

"She's cool man," said Eric.

"She's really pretty Ryan, way to go buddy," I yelled down. I wanted to tell him to hold on to his wallet. "She may not eat, but at least she pees, so she's human," I joked.

"Aww...we've only been out a few times, but I really think I like her."

"Oooh yay, can I be your flower girl?" I asked laughing.

"Sure thing Vada," Ryan smiled.

Well hell. I sat there thinking, so what if she's all decked out, and overdone, and completely stupid? He likes her. She likes him. Why should I be so judgmental? We actually got to watch the game for a moment in peace, and then I looked up and saw her making her way down the stairs, brushing off her dress like there were flies around her. I hate flies. She made her way to the seat. Apparently, we were paying musical chairs because Ryan scooted down, so it went Ryan, Trinity, Eric, and me, next to a rather serious spectator who didn't take his eyes off the game. I should have just come with him.

"So, what did I miss?" said Trinity.

Oh WTF? There it was as clear as day. The non-eating, perfectly-chic-fabulously-fit glam-girl had ketchup and mustard smeared on the top of her plump upper lip. She had just gone up and slammed down a tube steak and forgot to wipe off the evidence. The "flies" must have been bun crumbs she was brushing off her dress. I don't think the guys had noticed yet.

Okay, I had two options here. I could have either not said a thing and let her look like a fool, or I could hand her a napkin and keep it our little secret. Shit. I hate being in these situations. Having to make a quick decision, I looked at Eric who had already noticed. His eyes were open wide and he was almost about to bust out with the laughter that he was trying to hold inside. I gave him my shut the fuck up look and he pretended to cough. In a split decision, I did the unthinkable. I grabbed her face with two hands, hell at least *I* had used hand sanitizer before touching someone's face. I leaned in and whispered, "This is our other little secret okay? But take this napkin and wipe that shit off your face before Ryan sees it. Your secret is safe with me."

She immediately did some delicate *achoos* into the napkin that sounded like princess sneezes and got rid of the evidence. She whispered thank you.

We watched the rest of the game pretty much in silence. It was a good game at least.

On the way home that night, I realized that I may have done that girl a favor, but if she was really planning on settling down, she better get a little more real. Shit, if she's not willing to eat a hotdog in front of him, how is she ever going to take a shit if they get married? Is she going to run down to the gas station every day? What if she gets pregnant and has lots of gas? Then when she gives birth he has to watch her vagina expand ten centimeters and push a baby out, and she may crap on the table. That's when shit gets real. It made me appreciate that Eric and I may not be perfect, but we are real. We really know and love each other. Whether those two end up together or not, only time will tell. But in the meantime at least she has gotten to enjoy his money and a really good wiener.

Morning Madness

I've been in seven times now
I have tried to wake you up
Your cereal is waiting
And your juice is in your cup
So get your butts in gear now
We must leave in half an hour
Quick go brush your teeth
And get yo' asses in the shower
I kindly packed your lunches
I laid out your favorite clothes
Now don't you fucking tell me
You don't feel like wearing those
You have to move your bodies
I can't carry you to school
Your backpacks will not pack themselves
Don't make me lose my cool
I said you can't play Minecraft
We are going to be late
No Xbox and no coloring
It's almost freaking eight
I don't know where your socks are
Now please go and find your shoes
Why are you waiting til right now
to take your morning poos?
I'm waiting in the car for you
So hurry up and go
Does every morning have to be
a god-awful shit show?
Okay you're done, get in the car
And buckle up real fast
I hope you guys have awesome days
I hope you have a blast
Why do you look so sad my loves?
I'll miss you all day too

Now get your asses out my car
Your mom's got shit to do
We kiss goodbye I drive away
I feel a twinge of sadness
I always miss those crazy kids
Despite our morning madness

~ I thought I'd write a poem while it was fresh in my mind on this glorious
Monday morning. What a good time it was writing that shit. Now I have to
go back up to the school, because Max left his effing backpack in the car. I
mean...really???

Happy Anniversary

I came home from getting the boys from school yesterday and found a note on my door. It was from Sweet Bouquets. It looked like it must be a flower shop here in town. I grabbed the pretty pink slip and noticed that there was a box checked that read:

SORRY WE MISSED YOU, WE'LL TRY AGAIN TOMORROW

What did he do? Why did he send flowers? And then it hit me. It was our anniversary and I had forgotten all about it. I felt like a total douche. Not really because I care that much about anniversaries, but because I hate being wrong. I hate having to admit mistakes. Shit! I knew he would be home soon, so I didn't have much time.

Good thing I'm a fucking genius, because I had a brilliant idea! I corralled my little precious angel boys into the house and sat them all down at the table. I got out our bucket of art supplies and told them that this was Mommy and Daddy's special day, and that I needed them to help make something for Daddy. They all had their assignments, even Jordan. They got busy, and so did I. I went to the storage room and immediately went into motion, like a rescue worker into rubble to find just the right pictures.

When I say, I went into motion, I mean I destroyed that bitch. Trusting the kids with art supplies while I am not in the room is not something I would normally do, but desperate times call for desperate measures, and I was NOT going to be the one to come up short on this anniversary crap. Flowers my ass! I was making a homemade gift from the children, so Eric...top that muthafucka! I found a baby picture of each of the boys, and one picture of Eric and me from our trip to Nassau on our honeymoon. I ignored the undeniable fact that this trip sucked lamb balls.

Our honeymoon had been a bust for a few reasons. First off, I was having the period from hell, which I do every time I have ever gone on vacation in my life! Secondly, all Eric wanted to do was stay in the hotel room and watch Jerry Springer reruns. What a great way to spend time in the

Bahamas. Eric has always thought that vacations were meant to be spent relaxing. I remember telling him he was the lamest man that I had ever married. I actually also told him (after a pitcher of margaritas that I drank by myself on the hotel room balcony) that on my next honeymoon I was going to go somewhere way nicer with a six-packed underwear model with a schlong the size of my forearm which also had a surgically implanted vibrating switch installed in the shaft. But for now, it has been my only honeymoon and I looked kind of good in that picture, so I grabbed it anyway and ran back to the kids, leaving the storage room looking like a crime scene. I grabbed a couple rolls of wrapping paper and hauled ass back up to the minions.

By this time the kitchen was a mess, but I didn't care because my eye was on the prize. The boys did exactly as I had asked them to, for once! Ben had drawn a picture of me and Eric, and Max had drawn a picture of him and his two brothers. I couldn't help but laugh at the picture of Eric and me that Ben had drawn. I had very large oval shaped knockers that looked like they were growing out of my armpits and Eric had the tiniest head I had ever seen and was wearing what appeared to be some sort of pilgrim hat. I ran up and grabbed an old collage picture frame out from under my bed and removed the matting and photos that had been occupying the forgotten and dust-covered, but decently cute, frame. I laid down some wrapping paper, choosing white with gold stars because it was the only one that didn't have a cartoon character, or a balloon, on it. I situated the pictures in a manner that would appear they had a rhyme or reason, but in reality I just spread them out, even the little scribbles that Jordan made. It looked pretty damn good if I do say so myself. I was going to look on Pinterest for some clever little romantic saying, but there was no time for bullshit. Besides...he's a guy, so words are pretty much as useless as an appendix. I stood back, admired our creation, and then ran back up to my room for the finishing touch. I changed into a little pair of Superwoman under britches (boy shorts, that's how I roll) and a lacy red bra that I only wear before I beg Eric to let me buy something expensive, like my new dishwasher this past August. I threw on a short white silk robe and checked my nose for any unsexy danglers. I lined my lips and put on some deep red lipstick that I had bought last Christmas for Eric's company party, powdered my face to even out the stress splotches from the day, and swiped a few strokes of mascara on the ol' eye batters. It still wasn't slutty enough, so I pulled a trick out of my hat...a Crayola washable marker in royal blue. I opened my robe up and did the sluttiest thing I've done yet in my marriage. I drew a downward arrow from just below my belly button pointing down to my lady bits, and I wrote a message that I thought was perfect. I couldn't believe how bold I was being. I felt like a dirty whore for the first time in my life, and I actually wanted to feel that way. I mean, I've still been testing out my new boobies, which I just got a few months ago. For some reason, something had clicked and I instantly felt like I had my sexy back. I was actually getting into this for once. I'm not really into flowers, but who knew what surprise he would come home with? I knew that no matter whether it was jewelry, or a tiny white Persian kitten with a crystal-encrusted collar, nothing could top the excitement, or anticipation, of Super-Ho Vada, and I was going to blow his mind. We usually have about twenty-three minutes of alone time between the time the kids fall asleep, and the time they come running back up to our room in a state of panic because they've been left alone. I did a twirl in the mirror and when I turned around I noticed Max standing there in my doorway. I quickly closed my robe and tied it. That kid is like having an extra shadow that follows me around, and talks and poops.

"Mommy, did you draw on your tummy? Can I do it too?"

I was busted, but for that one moment I was glad he wasn't an advanced reader, he had no idea what it said. I knew it was better if I played along.

"Ben! Bring Jordan up here! We are coloring our tummies!" I yelled.

After letting them "tattoo" each other to the point of ridiculousness, I called Papa John's Pizza and waited for Eric to get home. Unfortunately, the pizza guy came to the door before Eric did, so I kind of felt like a porn star answering the door in my white robe, but the kids took the edge off. I lit a candle and set out plates. I heard the door click and in walked Eric. He was carrying a cup of coffee without a lid that he must have left in his car before work. It spilled all over the floor and he took his shoes off by the front door. I wanted to start screaming at him and smash the coffee cup over his head, but it was a special day. Instead, I bit my lip and walked to greet him with a Clorox wipe, pecked a smooch, and wiped up the mess before it could get sticky.

Sitting down to eat pizza with the family, I expected him to say something about my robe, but he didn't. I wasn't going to let that bother me though. I was more disappointed that he didn't mention my porn lips. WTF? I was looking pretty smokin' if you ask me, but he was stuffing his face with pizza. He hadn't even said Happy Anniversary. I figured he was waiting until he pulled a jewelry box out of his pocket or something. The room around me was filled with the sounds of sloppy chews and requests for drink refills. As the kids slowed down and started to squirm I decided that it was time to acknowledge my flowers. I knew he would be disappointed that they wouldn't be here until tomorrow and I wanted to smooth it over.

"Eric, I want to tell you that I love you like crazy. Don't get upset, but I just missed the delivery guy that came to drop off my flowers today, but they are coming back tomorrow. Thank you so much for the thought honey, that's the most important thing. I really do love you and it's been such a wonderful eight years, except for maybe a couple here and there, however the majority has been great. Happy Anniversary!" I said. I actually meant it. What the fuck was happening to me? I felt like I wanted to have sex with him later and that never fucking happens. Eric sat there looking at me and his lip was shaking. It always shakes when he's nervous. I felt bad for him that his surprise for me didn't come, but like I said, it was the thought that counted.

"Happy Anniversary Vadie girl," he said and leaned over to kiss me. "That's not all I have for you, you know." I knew it!!!

"The kids worked really hard to make you something today. So boys, let's show Daddy!"

Jordan stayed on Eric's lap and the two big boys went in with me and they each carried a side of the picture frame with their masterpiece inside.

"Happy Birthday Dad," said Max.

"It's not his birthday," said Ben. "It's the day Daddy peed on Mommy and grew babies in her tummy."

Oh for the love of John Stamos, where the hell did he hear that? "Boys, it's the day Mom and Dad got married! Seven years ago today. It's called an anniversary. Babies come later," I explained.

"Why did Daddy pee on you? Like he had to water your baby? Did he pee on all of us?" asked Max.

"No, Daddy never peed on me. Babies don't need to be watered like that," I explained, hoping Eric would chime in and help me out...but he didn't. "Let's give him his gift guys."

Eric finally got his ass off his chair and crouched down to the floor, setting Jordan down to fuss over the picture. "Thank you guys! I love it. This is too cool!" He hugged them all and then kissed me and subtly grabbed my ass.

"I'll pee on you if you want," he whispered.

I rolled my eyes. "Now, one more thing," I said. "Let's show Daddy our tattoos!"

The boys lifted their shirts up revealing their artwork that had smudged a little bit, but looked cute. They were so proud and I was content with how things were going. I asked the boys to run in and put their jammies on. I was going to let them skip their baths so they could keep their tattoos and I was going to let them play a little longer, then go to bed early. As soon as they left the room, I gave Eric my sexy look, which I assume is sexy, but in reality, it probably looks more like a constipated look, and told him I had a tattoo to show him too. I opened up my robe revealing my super-stripper attire and my washable marker letters and arrow that read:

ENTER HERE
AN INCH +1 FOR EACH YEAR
HAPPY ANNIVERSARY

His eyes about popped out of his head and his jaw dropped to his chest. You would have thought he'd never seen a chick in her under britches before. I couldn't believe what I was doing. He didn't say a word, just kissed me hard and held my face in his hands. One hand went down my stomach and then to the baby shoot.

"Not yet you stupid! The kids will be back in here in about two seconds!"

"You can't do that to me and not give it up Vadie. That's false advertising!" He sounded like a whiny baby.

"Okay then, let's traumatize the living shit out of them, shall we? Then you can explain to Child Protective Services that you just couldn't wait, while I hire an attorney to regain custody of our children after the boys go to school and tell their guidance counselor what they have seen."

"Vadie, shit. Well, let's get the kids to bed early. It hurts."

"You're funny."

"No, I'm horny."

We went through the motions of the night and the boys repeatedly begged for five more minutes, and every time I agreed, Eric would shoot me a death glare. He looked so desperate I almost worried he was going to grab his keys, drive up to the grocery store, run into the bakery, pull out a glazed donut from the display case, and screw it right there in the middle of the aisle without paying for it. Eww. I finally felt bad enough for him that I ended the boys' stalling tactics and tucked them into bed. Jordan went right to sleep and Eric was pacing in the hallway. What a dork. At least I felt desirable for once. Chicks need that sometimes.

After the final set of child eyes were closed, I tip-toed up the stairs and found Eric sitting straight up on the end of the bed. It almost looked like he had a board on his back and he was frozen stiff, in more ways than one. I asked him to hold on because I wanted to grab my phone. I knew that if it rang, it would wake the kids. I ran down and pulled it from the charger on the kitchen counter, but I noticed the glowing screen showing that I had received a text. I immediately recognized the phone number as my mother-in-law's.

WANTED TO MAKE SURE YOU GOT THE ARRANGEMENT I SENT TODAY,
LOVE, MARILYN AND FRANK

Well bend me over and tickle my flaps. He never sent me a damn thing after all! That sonofabitch forgot our anniversary. I was fuming. Not only did he forget, but he was trying to take credit for his mother's kind gesture. I could have strangled him. By that point, the fact that I too had forgotten this day, meant jack shit to me. I had already busted my ass to make up for it. I wrote a pornographic message on my stomach, which even flattered him with an extra inch, and assisted our offspring in creating a beautiful fucking art piece with priceless sentimental value.

I stood there in the hallway for a moment trying to decide what to do. I concluded that he must pay for this, one way or another. I made a trip back down to the fridge and grabbed a bottle of chocolate syrup, and a can of sprayable Cool Whip. This is definitely something I have never done before, and I normally hate sticky things, but I needed these weapons. With my hands full, I shimmied up my bra so that the girls were as high and delightful as humanly possible. In fact, if I would have looked down I probably would have suffocated. Eric is definitely a boob guy, so these were literally my "big-guns." I started back up to our bedroom and shook my robe off, letting it fall to the floor. I took a deep breath in, to suck in my stomach of course. As I entered the room, Eric looked as excited as a *Star Trek* geek in a brothel. His eyes were huge, and he already had his jeans unzipped. Poor dude. I shut the door behind me, set my phone and dessert toppings on my dresser, which I couldn't help but notice needed a good dusting, and then I walked over to him.

"What the hell has gotten into you Vadie? I mean, I really like it, so whatever it is, keep doing it."

I held his hands in my face and smiled, "Well kid, I just thought I'd surprise you. I have to admit, I can't believe you remembered our anniversary today without even having to remind you. Impressive."

"Of course I remembered baby. What are you going to do with that stuff?" he asked. The anticipation was plastered on his face. I began to wonder if the poor guy needed to get a girlfriend.

"Well...let me show you," I said trying hard not to bust out laughing. I grabbed the chocolate syrup and Cool Whip and decorated his privacy until it looked just like a fucking banana split, complete with nuts and all. I've never actually had one though; I am extremely allergic to bananas. The only thing missing was a cherry on top, but who the hell has a cherry lying around?

He just lay there, leaning back on his elbows and staring at me like he couldn't figure out if it was all a dream, a really delicious and moist dream. I took a step back and admired my work, although it did look rather sticky and I don't do well with messes. I resisted the nagging urge to lunge for the baby wipes. At least that shit wasn't on *me*. I would probably start convulsing if I had that gluey crap on my lady flesh. I shook off the idea and nonchalantly walked back over to the dresser and picked up my phone. Eric just laid there in pure amazement. I was starting to feel kind of bad. I mean, I am normally such a prudish old bore in the sack, always saying things like, *don't touch that! go wash your hands!* and *I said don't look at it!* It occurred to me that maybe I should ditch my plan of getting him all revved up, and then pulling the plug at the last minute, so he could think about what he'd done. That actually *was* my original plan. But gazing into his eyes I saw my husband looking at me in a different light, like I was some sort of sex goddess or something. In fact, I kind of felt like one. Who the hell does things like this? I mean I was behaving like a total tramp...and

I liked it! I mean, Anna Steele had nothing on Vada Bower. I had made up my mind; I would get him to spill the beans and then forgive him, and then carry on with this love fest. I was freaking out about the sticky sweet part, and kind of regretting how much Cool Whip I had used, but hell, I could pop a Xanax to take the edge off and try something new for once. This Missionary Princess was going to trade in her crown and become the next Blow Job Betty. Only first, I at least wanted him to fess up. Then, I was going to star in my very first kinky lay.

"Hmm...Lovey, before we go any further...do you have anything you need to tell me?"

"Uh, yeah. I like this."

"I know you do, but do you have anything that you need to get off your chest? Seriously babe, I'll forgive you. I already figured it out. Just tell me the truth." He looked so busted.

"Vadie listen, I think I know what you're talking about. Honey, I can explain. I…"

"Eric, you don't have to explain. Just say it. I already told you that I'll forgive you. I know anyway. Look at me. I swear. I heard from your mom."

"You did?"

"She texted me."

"Okay, I know you are talking about yesterday. I slept for a while. I was going to go to work, but I just needed a day. I didn't want to tell you because I thought you'd be mad. I'm sorry Vadie."

Was I hearing this correctly? What was he talking about? Whatever was this verbal vomit I heard spewing from my husband's mouth? Did he just say he took a day off yesterday? He slept? I remember him kissing me goodbye and leaving for work. I remember it. He lied to me! I felt my cheeks start to fill up with that reddish ragey shit that happens when a girl's just about to start slappin' a bitch. I was trying to figure out if I was piecing all of this together correctly.

"Eric," I started.

"No Vadie. I'm sorry. I was wrong for doing that. It's just that I've had a bad cold. I knew if I stayed home I wouldn't get any rest here. So I went to my parents' house and took some NyQuil and slept. I should have told you. I just needed a sick day."

"You have a cold? A cold? Are you fucking kidding me? I had three children, you shitface! Go count them. That is twenty-seven months of pregnancy! That is three C-section deliveries, plus fifteen hours of pointless labor that I had to go through to even get to the first C-section!" I was shouting. "That was bleeding and cracked nipples on top of engorged tits with bouts of mastitis. That was not drinking alcohol, and not eating lunch meat, and not sleeping, and being constipated, and getting fat...really freaking fat every single time, and then having to try desperately to lose the weight, and then having people judge the way I looked in clothes when they were pretending to be looking at my babies! That was leg cramps, and itching, and having a gynecologist shove gloved fingers into my cervix when I was so goddamn swollen that it sounded like a fucking squeegee coming out of there, and then getting a giant Q-tip shoved up my ass to test me for some random bacteria that I always conveniently had so I had to take antibiotics, and then got yeast infections from it. That was blood, sweat, and tears bro, and not once, I mean not *once*, did I get a sick day."

"I thought you said you were going to forgive me?" he said.

"I meant that you forgot our anniversary! Oh geez Eric, and by the way Eric, you didn't send me flowers! Your mother did!"

"Oh my God Vadie, I said I'm sorry. I admit that I forgot our anniversary. I have really messed this whole thing up, haven't I? I told you I had something else for you."

238

"Okay, then what is it?" I said. My hands were in the air like I was at a rock concert.

Eric looked at the wall. He wouldn't look me in the eye. I knew he was full of shit. He was probably going to run out for coffee in the morning, and stop at Walmart and get me some stupid slippers or something. He looked really sad. But who does that? Who leaves for work and goes and sleeps at their mother's house? I wanted to call Marilyn and ask her if she was planning on covering up this lie. I was too pissed to think clearly, so I just went and grabbed my robe and put it back on.

"Damn it Vada, are you just going to leave me here like this on our anniversary?" Eric asked. He laid there still frozen with an ice cream sundae on his floppy disc. "Can't you just forgive me and we can get back to what we were doing? I've learned my lesson and I am really, really sorry!"

I leaned down and put one hand on his chest. I licked my lips and could taste the lipstick I had slathered on. "Sorry baby, I'll forgive you, but I will not touch you, and you are sleeping downstairs."

"Why? Why can't we just do this?"

"Well honey, from what you told me, you have a terrible cold...and I don't want to get sick. Now go clean up and get your ass down on the couch. You need your rest." I walked into our master bathroom and shut the door. I showered and put on my old frumpster pajamas and crawled into bed alone. He followed directions and slept on the couch.

That night I cried a little bit before I fell asleep. I realized the only one who had remembered our anniversary was my mother-in-law and that made me kind of sad. I wish romance was more of a priority. Then and there, I set a goal to make it one. I felt he had been punished enough and we could eventually get past this.

I woke up this morning early and was traveling through my normal daily routine, when I heard the doorbell ring. When I answered it, I saw a little man who looked like a grandpa vampire, if there was ever such a thing. He had a widow's peak and canines that could eat a T-bone without utensils. I was confused when he handed me a big bouquet of fruit. It was one of those arrangements with the fruit all shaped like flowers and the tall round vase had a big red bow around it. I thanked the little bloodsucker and set the arrangement down on the table. There was a sticky note attached to little card on the top, I pulled it out and read the apology that the delivery service missed us yesterday. Then, I opened the little envelope on that little stick that I'm always worried the kids will poke their eyes out on. Here is what it said:

HOPE YOU FEEL BETTER SOON ERIC. PLEASE GET SOME REST.
LOVE, YOUR MOTHER

I set my head in my hands, realizing that my mother-in-law hadn't sent me flowers after all. She sent her son some fucking fruit because he had been faking sick at her house. Well screw it. I guess no one remembered this year. I glanced over the pineapples, orange slices and strawberries on skewers. I pulled out a banana and two melon balls and placed them in the shape of a wanker and laughed to myself. It may be immature, but I still think it's funny. Then I decided to do one more thing. I picked out all of the fruit that I liked, put it on a plate and covered it in Cool Whip and chocolate sauce. I picked out a cherry, put it on top, and ate the shit out of it. It was really effing delicious. I left Eric a plain banana. What can I say? I'm allergic to bananas.

~Vada

Showers...?

Instead of having bridal showers, there should be "We've been married for seven years and now all of our shit is breaking and wearing out at the same time, so we have to replace every fucking thing in our house we and could really use a little help here" showers. Just a thought...

Just Beat It

Thinking I was an effing genius, I signed Ben up for an after school basketball camp. Being 6 years-old, I thought he should get a little experience before I throw him on a team. I knew a few of my friends' kids would be going and so I felt good about it. The van from the local kids sports club was going to pick him up from school and it was supposed to start yesterday and run until Friday, so five days of basketball bliss...right?

I had everything situated and worked it out with the school that Ben would be picked up in the regular pick-up line. I got a call from the school principal, Mrs. Funk, around ten minutes after dismissal. The woman talks like she is literally sitting in a swiveling chair with a giant stick in the center of the seat so that it is submerged right up into her ass. Ugh...I just want to be like lighten up woman! You work with children, but at least they go home! Anyway, her pissy voice squeals through my phone, "Mrs. Bower, we seem to have a situation."

Panicked, I quickly asked, "What's going on?"

"Benjamin's transportation is confusing to the staff and I told the driver that she needs to be waiting in the regular bus line."

"Okay Mrs. Funk. I will let them know when I pick him up from camp that they need to go to the bus line from now on. Ben made it though, right? Everything's okay?"

"Well, I already told the driver that today. It's not okay, because we can't release children in vehicles when they are not in the proper lines. Yes Benjamin made it, but tomorrow I'm sending him to the bus line."

"Well, thank you Mrs. Funk. I will make sure to remind them."

"Like I said, I already told them. Have a good evening."

She clicked the phone down before I could tell her to fuck off. I never actually would have said it, but still, why bother calling me? I'd bet she bobs up and down on her ass rod. I brushed it off and accepted that she was just a bitch and went about my business. I picked up Ben from basketball camp and he had a blast! Seriously, he loved it! Thank goodness because it cost more than a pap smear without insurance. Last night I told Eric about the old haggy principal and he made some disgusting joke about her vagina probably being cold and moth-eaten and we chuckled and then forgot about it.

Today, the dismissal time had passed and I didn't receive a phone call. I was relieved, at least until Eric called.

"Oh shit Vadie!"

"What's wrong?" I asked.

"Oh man I just fucked up!"

"What did YOU DO?" I yelled.

"Well, that old bitch principal just emailed me and said that Ben's ride was in the wrong line again and she told me that next time this happens that they will not release him out of the school's custody."

"Geez Eric, calm down," I said relieved. "What's the big deal? We'll just remind them again."

"No Vadie, you don't understand. I was meaning to forward the email on to you, but I accidentally did something wrong."

Oh fuck. "Just tell me...make it quick. What did you DO?"

"I accidentally hit reply instead of forward."

"So?"

"Well, I thought I was sending it to YOU, so I wrote on there that if she didn't release my son, I would beat that bitch's ass."

Oh holy humping hedgehogs. "Oh God! Eric you idiot!"

"I know. I know. I'm freaking out," he said. "Oh crap, the other line is beeping in, I'll call you back.

All I could do was vacuum. This wasn't really happening right? I mean, my kids are all going to have to go to school there for the next decade! WTF? Jordan was making me hold him while I cleaned every nook and cranny of that motherfucking house. I tried calling Eric back and got no answer. Finally, I loaded up Max and Jordan and went to pick up Ben from camp.

Of course he had a blast and so that made me happy, but I chewed every one of my tiny brittle fingernails off on the way home. I saw Eric's car in the driveway as I turned the corner. I held my breath and walked inside with my babies. He was sitting on the couch with his light blue button down shirt halfway unbuttoned, and he looked unwell. His hair was a mess and he was tapping his leg.

"So?" I asked. "What happened? Who called you?"

"Well, let me explain. I never got a chance to tell you this, but I emailed her immediately after I realized what I had done, and asked her not to open that email. I told her that it was meant for someone else."

"Oh God Eric, of course she was going to open it if you said that!"

"Yeah, and then I got a call from the police department because she said she felt threatened."

Luckily, the kids were not listening as they had immediately walked in and started on their electronics. Holy crap. What the hell was I going to do? "Eric, what did you say?"

"I told the truth and said she is an evil woman. I told them when I said, beat her ass, I meant like kick her ass, not actually beat it."

"WHAT? What are you fucking Michael Jackson or something? Who cares if you beat it or kick it? You seriously told the police that you just wanted to kick her ass?"

"No, I mean like I was just saying it as an expression, not an actual threat. I already feel stupid enough, okay? Don't make it worse. "

"Oh no Eric...I'm not going to make it worse. You are going to pick them up every single livelong day for the rest of the year. How am I supposed to volunteer up there now, huh? God, are we even allowed back there?"

"Yes, yes it's fine. Just trust me. It's fine."

"Whatever MJ. I'm going to wear a mask when I go up for the next school function and seriously, all communication with that bitch must now go through you...or your defense attorney."

We went on about our normal night and now the kids are asleep. Eric finally calmed down. We realized that if he was going to be arrested, they would've come by now. Phew! I can't help but laugh. She is quite a troll and I wasn't ever mad at him for writing it, just sending it to HER! Oh well. Maybe she won't cause such a shit fit over the bus line anymore. I think Eric's going to try to sleep with me tonight for comfort reasons. Poor guy needs to feel better. But you know what? I'm too tired, so he can just beat it.

Got My Hair Did

How much it costs to get my hair highlighted, lowlighted, and cut: $185.98

How much the boxed shimmery brown hair color costs to fix it because it's way too blonde for me: $9.98

How it makes me feel when no one, not even my husband notices I ever did a thing to my hair: WORTHLESS

I Can't Look

When I look at the loves of my life walking through my house, I see walking laundry. When I look at the water my kids drink, I see piss stains around the toilet that I know I will eventually be cleaning up. When I look at someone in my family eating something, all I can see are crumbs. When I look at chocolate, all I can see is my ass getting wider. When I look at my bed when I crawl into it at night, all I can see is that it needs to be made in the morning. When I look at the mail, all I can see is that there are bills that need to be paid. When I look at my life, it sometimes seems like a cycle that I just can't keep up with. So I will now walk around with a blindfold on so I can't see anything. That is, unless John Stamos is on TV. Then I will look.

Thoughts for the Day...

I seriously think I'm going to end up in a mental institution one of these days. My kids are driving me crazy! That is all.

MY FAIRY TALE

Once upon a time, there was a girl named Vada. She lived in a gigantic eight-bedroom house that included six bathrooms, a movie theater, a kitchen that would make Emeril cum in his chef pants, and a staff of nine, including two housekeepers, two security guards, a masseuse, a chef, a bartender, a hair and makeup artist, and last but not least, a scrumptious looking lifeguard that would perch his rock-hard ass on a chair and watch over her while she lay her svelte and sculpted body on a lounge chair soaking up the sun that never caused her a single wrinkle. Her three amazing children spoke two languages, and already had scholarships to Ivy League schools while still attending elementary and pre-K. She didn't need a gym because she had a metabolism that worked as fast as one of those disturbingly odd looking speed skaters that compete in the Olympic Games.

Yes, life was good for Vada. Her husband Eric had a job that afforded her a life of luxury. After a hard day's work, he'd come home and kiss her; an open-mouth kiss that you would imagine happening at the end of a romantic movie. This happened each and every day. Then, he would play ball with the kids and do "dad" things like arm wrestling, and being a good role model, and shit. After they ate a delicious sit-down full service meal, complete with wine and white chocolate raspberry cheesecake on a nightly basis, they got their precious little offspring tucked safely into their beds, Eric would carry her into their bedroom, to a bed scattered with fresh yellow rose petals. It is in this glorious bed that he repeatedly pleasured her as he did every night, while asking for nothing in return. She then slept for ten uninterrupted hours and the next morning, she woke , opened her eyes, and stretched her arms up in a glorious release. Once she blinked a few times and looked at the digital alarm clock, she realized that it was only two-thirty in the morning and her toddler was wailing through the monitor. Vada flung the covers off, looked over at her husband who was pretending not to hear the baby. She growled, told him to enjoy the fucking sleep that he was faking, and went to put the sweet baby back to sleep. Only, it took her little lovey three hours to finally close his eyes. Finally, at five-thirty Vada crawled back in her bed and lay there anxiously until her two older children woke up at six o'clock. And everyone lived happily ever after, except for Vada, because she was too tired to actually classify as being alive. The End

Crazy Mother

Oh why is it so loud in here?
I can't hear myself think
I know that you need help with that
Your brother wants a drink
If I step on one more Lego
I may vacuum them all up
The baby just fell off the chair
He spilled his pudding cup
Who colored on the freaking wall?
And who forgot to flush?
Will I ever even get a chance
To play my Candy Crush?
I sometimes stop and wonder
How the hell will I get through?
Can I do this for another day?
I don't know what to do
But then those moments happen
When we stop and hug each other
There's no one I would rather be
Than these kids' Crazy Mother

THE END

Thank you for reading. Join me on my blog at theminivanprincess.com for more crazy shit!

CPSIA information can be obtained
at www.ICGtesting.com
Printed in the USA
LVHW021758300119
605775LV00001B/139/P